Magnolia

Jorge Consuegra

OVER BLACK;
NARRATOR
In the New York Herald, November 26, year 1911, there is an account of the hanging
of three men --

CUT TO:
Black and White Lumiere Footage
Three men hung....bang...bang...bang.

CUT TO:
Newspaper Headline comes into focus; "Three Men Hung."

QUICK DISSOLVE:
Sub Head comes into focus; "...for murder of..."

CUT TO:
INT. APARTMENT/FOYER - EVENING (Lumiere Footage Contd.)
A man in period dress (1911) walks in the door. CAMERA DOLLIES IN QUICK as he
takes his hat off, shakes snow, looks off --

NARRATOR
...they died for the murder of Sir Edmund William Godfrey -- Sir Edmund is greeted by
his WIFE and two CHILDREN.

NARRATOR
-- Husband, Father, Pharmacist and all around gentle-man resident of --

CUT TO:
EXT. STREET - NIGHT
CAMERA pushes in on the town sign, reads:
"Greenberry Hill, London. Population 1276"

NARRATOR
Greenberry Hill, London. Population as listed.

CUT TO:
EXT. PHARMACY - NIGHT
HIGH ANGLE, looking down as Sir Edmond comes out the door, locks up for the
evening. CAMERA BOOMS DOWN and PUSHES IN

TOWARDS HIM, WHIPS RT TOWARDS:
NARRATOR
He was murdered by three vagrants whose motive was simple robbery. They were
identified as:
A COATED MAN standing in the shadows of the alley way nearby.

NARRATOR
...Joseph Green.....
CAMERA WHIPS RT. again, nearby ANOTHER MAN steps closer --

NARRATOR
...Stanley Berry....
CAMERA WHIPS RT. one more time and PUSH IN towards THE LAST MAN --

NARRATOR
...and Nigel Hill...

WIDE ANGLE, ABOVE SCENE.
The three men move in on Sir Edmond and start to knife him to death, stealing his money and jewelry. CAMERA PULLS BACK and up to include the sign of the pharmacy now:
"Greenberry Hill Pharmacy."

CUT TO:
LUMIERE FOOTAGE REPLAYED.
Three men hug. Bang...bang...bang...

NARRATOR
Green, Berry and Hill.
FREEZE FRAME On the last hanging image.

NARRATOR
...And I Would Like To Think This Was Only A Matter Of Chance.

OPTICAL WIPE OF FLAMES FILL THE SCREEN, CAMERA PULLS BACK:
EXT. FORREST/NEAR LAKE TAHOE - NIGHT (35mm/color/anamorphic now)
CAMERA is in the midst of a large FORREST FIRE. CAMERA

WHIPS RT TO SEE:
THREE FIREMEN battling the flames. CAMERA PUSHES IN On them as they scream and shout directions at each other:

NARRATOR
As reported in the Reno Gazzette, June of 1983 there is the story of a fire ---

HIGH ANGLE, THE TREE TOPS.
The trees are on fire....moments later....

NARRATOR
--- the water that it took to contain the fire --

WATER FALLS DOWN...

dropped from a FIRE DEPARTMENT AIR TANKER.

CUT TO:
EXT. FORREST/NEAR LAKE TAHOE - MORNING
CAMERA pushes in towards FOUR FIREFIGHTERS as they survey the area. The fire is out and they are walking through. The MAIN FIREFIGHTER steps into a close up and looks:

NARRATOR
-- and a scuba diver named Delmer Darion.

FIREFIGHTER'S POV, THAT MOMENT
CAMERA dollies in and TILTS up towards the top of the tree to reveal:
There is a MAN IN SCUBA GEAR hanging high in the tree.
He is wearing his goggles and his tanks and his wet suit.

FIRE FIGHTER (OC)
What the fuck is that?

ANGLE, CU. DELMER DARION.
He still has his mask and mouthpiece.

CUT TO:
INT. PEPPERMILL CASINO - NIGHT - FLASHBACK
CAMERA looks down on a blackjack game, BOOM DOWN and TILT UP to reveal:
DELMER DARION (40s)

NARRATOR
Employee of the Peppermill Hotel and Casino, Reno, Nevada. Engaged as a blackjack dealer --

CUT TO:
INT. CASINO/LOBBY - EARLY MORNING – FLASHBACK CAMERA pushes in towards Delmer as he leaves for the nght, his uniform draped on a hanger over his shoulder, he nods and motions two fingers to his fellow WORKERS who say "so longer."
(Note: He has a bandage over his forehead.)

NARRATOR
-- well liked and well regarded as a physical, recreational and sporting sort --
Delmer's true passion was for the lake --

CUT TO:
INT. LAKE TAHOE/UNDERWATER - DAY
Delmer SPLASHES in and comes down towards the CAMERA. SOUND drops out, becomes very quiet...

CUT TO:
EXT. LAKE TAHOE - THAT MOMENT
The FIRE DEPARTMENT AIR TANKER comes flying in, heading towards the lake, coming directly at CAMERA...

CUT TO:
INT. LAKE TAHOE/UNDERWATER - THAT MOMENT
Delmer dives. Silent and peaceful.

CUT TO:
EXT. LAKE TAHOE - THAT MOMENT
OVERHEAD ANGLE Looks down on the calm lake....beat, then:

THE MASSIVE AIR TANKER FILLS THE FRAME, TOUCHING DOWN ON THE WATER,
FULLING IT'S BODY FULL OF WATER FROM THE LAKE. It enters CAMERA RT. and exits CAMERA LFT.
ANGLE, THE AIR TANKER. It heads off full of water towards the raging forrest fire in the distance.

NARRATOR
-- as reported by the coroner, Delmer died of a heart attack somewhere between the lake and the tree. But most curious side note is the suicide the next day of Craig Hansen --

CUT TO:
EXT. RENO MOTEL - DAY - FLASHBACK
Establishing shot. (x3)

CUT TO:
INT. MOTEL - THAT MOMENT
CAMERA PUSHES IN SUPER QUICK towards a MAN named CRAIG HANSEN (30s)
He shoves a RIFLE under his chin and pulls the trigger, blood and brains splatter the ceiling.

CUT TO:
INT. AIR TANKER COCKPIT - FLASHBACK - DAY
HANSEN flying the plane. HOLD CU. as he moves towards the lake.

NARRATOR
...volunteer firefighter, estranged father of four and a poor tendency to drink -- Mr. Hansen was the pilot of the plane that quite accidentally lifted Delmer Darion out of the water --

CUT TO:

EXT. LAKE TAHOE - SHOT REPLAYED.
Quick flashback to the footage of the PLANE lifting the water from the lake, SOUND
CARRIES OVER....

CUT TO:
INT. CASINO - NIGHT - FLASHBACK
The Blackjack table where DELMER Is dealing. DOLLY AROUND to reveal a drunk
and obnoxious CRAIG HANSEN, screaming about the cards he's been dealt and
taunting Delmer

NARRATOR
-- added to this, Mr. Hansen's tortured life met before with
Delmer Darion just two nights previous --
Hansen SPITS and PUNCHES at Delmer Darion's FACE for dealing the cards he's been
dealt. SECURITY GUARDS attack and pull him to the ground.

CUT TO:
INT. MOTEL ROOM - DAY - BACK TO SCENE
CRAIG HANSEN reading the paper, looking at the cover story, that has a photo of
DELMER DARION. He's crying and mumbling to himself:

CRAIG HANSEN
...oh God...fuck...I'm sorry...I'm sorry...

NARRATOR
The weight of the guilt and the measure of coincidence so large,
Craig Hansen took his life.
Replay of Craig Hansen's suicide, except this time, right before he blows his head off
we hear him say, through tears:

CRAIG HANSEN
...forgive me...

CUT TO:
INT. CASINO - NIGHT - BACK TO SCENE
Back to the fight DELMER and CRAIG HANSEN are having: CAMERA DOLLIES
IN QUICK TOWARDS Delmer on the ground with blood coming from his nose.

FREEZE FRAME.
NARRATOR
And I Am Trying To Think This Was All
Only A Matter Of Chance.

QUICK DISSOLVE TO:
INSERT, CLOSE UP - HOTEL EVENTS BOARD.
It reads: Welcome! AAFS Awards Dinner and Reception

Walnut Room
8pm
INT. HOTEL BANQUET ROOM - NIGHT (1961)
CAMERA pushes in following two GUESTS through some double doors and reveals
the DINNER RECEPTION.

ANGLE, MAN BEHIND PODIUM.
CAMERA pushes in quick then blends to 60fps on a man in glasses:
DONALD HARPER, forensic scientist as he speaks into the microphone.

NARRATOR
The tale told at a 1961 awards dinner for the American Association Of Forensic
Science by Dr. Donald Harper, president of the association, began with a simple suicide
attempt --

CUT TO:
EXT. ROOFTOP - MORNING - FLASHBACK (1958).
A seventeen year old kid SYDNEY BARRINGER steps up on to the roof of a nine story
building and looks down.

NARRATOR
Seventeen year old Sydney Barringer.
In the city of Los Angeles on March 23, 1958.
CAMERA DOLLIES towards Sydney landing in a CLOSE UP of his feet on the ledge,
they wobble a bit -- he jumps, disappears from FRAME.
BEAT. The following happens very quickly:
ANGLE, looking up towards the sky...Sydney falls past CAMERA....
ANGLE, looking down towards the street...Sydney continues to fall...
ANGLE, a random window on the sixth floor of the building SMASHES....
ANGLE, Sydney's stomach...a BULLET rips into it as he falls...blood splatters and his
body flinches....
ANGLE, looking up towards the sky...Sydney's body and some shattered glass FALL
directly at the CAMERA...which pulls back a little to reveal: a SAFETY NET in the
foreground....Sydney's body falls LIMP into the net...FREEZE FRAME.

NARRATOR
The coroner ruled that the unsuccessful suicide had suddenly become a succesful
homicide. To explain:

CUT TO:
EXT. ROOFTOP - FLASHBACK.
Replay of shot. Sydney steps up on the rooftop. CAMERA pushes in towards him
quickly, this time moving into his COAT POCKET --

NARRATOR
The suicide was confirmed by a note, left in the breast pocket of Sydney Barringer --

DISSOLVE INTO:
INT. COAT POCKET - THAT MOMENT
CAMERA catches glimpses of the note, " I'm sorry..."
"...and in this time..." "...so I will go " "...and be with God..."

NARRATOR
At the same time young Sydney stood on the ledge of this nine story building, an argument swelled three stories below --

QUICK DISSOLVE TO:
INT. BUILDING/HALLWAY - THAT MOMENT
CAMERA pushes in towards the door of ROOM 638. We hear same screaming and yelling coming fram behind the door;

NARRATOR
The neighbors heard, as they usually did, the arguing of the tenants --

QUICK DISSOLVE TO:
INT. APARTMENT #638 - THAT MOMENT
An ELDERLY COUPLE (early 60s) are savagely fighting and throwing things. The OLDER MAN is backing away from the OLDER WOMAN who is coming at him with a SHOTGUN.

NARRATOR
-- and it was not uncommon for them to threaten each other with a shotgun or one of the many handguns kept in the house --

OLDER MAN
Put it down, put that fuckin' thing down Fay --

OLDER WOMAN
-- I'II fucking tell YOU. I'll shoot you in the face and end this argument and we see who's right --

NARRATOR
And when the shotgun accidentaly went off,
Sydney just happend to pass --
The OLDER WOMAN stumbles a bit on some furniture and the SHOTGUN goes off -- FIRES past the OLDER MAN's head -- and SMASHES the window behind him -- SYDNEY falls past and gets shot in the stomach, then falls out of FRAME -- (They're oblivious to this)

OLDER MAN
You CRAZY FUCKIN' BITCH WHAT ARE YOU DOING?

OLDER WOMAN
SHUT THE FUCK UP.
FREEZE FRAME on the two of them yelling and screaming:

NARRATOR
Added to this, the two tenants turned out to be: Fay and Arthur Barringer.
Sydney's mother and Sydney's father.

CUT TO:
INT. APARTMENT - DAY - LATER
CAMERA moves through the scene as POLICEMAN and DETECTIVES question the
OLDER COUPLE. Neighbors and lookie-loos around.

NARRATOR
When confronted with the charge, which took some figuring out for the officers on the
scene of the crime, Fay Barringer swore that she did not know that the gun was loaded.

FAY BARRINGER
I didn't know -- I didn't know --

ARTHUR BARRINGER
She always threatens me with the gun, but I don't keep it loaded --

DETECTIVE
-- and you didn't load the gun?

ARTHUR BARRINGER
Why would I load the gun?

CUT TO:
INT. APARTMENT/HALLWAY - THAT MOMENT
CAMERA moves through as OFFICERS are talking to and getting statements from
VARIOUS NEIGHBORS...CAMERA closes in on an EIGHT YEAR OLD BOY,
speaking with a DETECTIVE.

NARRATOR
A young boy who lived in the building, sometimes a vistor and friend to Sydney
Barringer said that he had seen, six days prior the loading of the shotgun --
The DETECTIVE turns his head and calls to another --

DETECTIVE
C'mere a minute --

CUT TO:
INT. APARTMENT - DAY - FLASHBACK.

CAMERA moves into a bedroom area where we see a FIGURE from the back sitting on the bed --

NARRATOR
It seems that the arguing and the fighting and all of the violence was far too much for Sydney Barringer and knowing his mother and father's tendency to fight, he decided to do something --
CAMERA reveals that it is Sydney Barringer who is loading the shotgun. The YOUNG BOY is sitting nearby, watching Sydney mumble to himself as he loads shells into the shotgun.

CUT TO:
INT. APARTMENT/HALLWAY - PRESENT
CAMERA moves in on the YOUNG BOY, who looks INTO CAMERA.

YOUNG BOY
He said he wanted them to kill each other, that all they wanted to do was kill each other and he would help them if that's what they wanted to do --

CUT TO:
EXT. BUILDING/ROOFTOP - DAY - FLASHBACK
This is a WIDE ANGLE REPLAY of the whole event. We see the whole building...Sydney starts to jump and the film suddenly slows down...
A diagram is made to reflect the narration...this is done like NFL coverage where the x's and o's and arrows and lines are drawn to indicate placement and moves, etc.)
An x appears on the top of the building over Sydney.

NARRATOR
Sydney Barringer jumps from the ninth floor rooftop --
His parents argue three stories below --
An o is marked to indicate their position. Image goes into MOTION with Sydney jumping...an ARROW is drawn that displays the PATH of his fall --

NARRATOR
Her accidental shotgun blast hits Sydney in the stomach as he passes the arguing sixth floor window --
Freeze Frame shows Sydney, hanging mid-air -- the glass shattering and starting to fall to the ground -- an X marks the spot where he is hit.

NARRATOR
He is killed instantly but continues to fall -- only to find, three stories below -- a safety net installed three days prior for a set of window washers that would have broken his fall and saved his life if not for the hole in his stomach.
A squiggly line with an arrow is drawn from Sydney to the net to indicate the path --
UNFREEZE frame and watch Sydney fall into the net

CUT TO:
INT. APARTMENT - DAY
CAMERA moves in on the PARENTS then over to some DETECTIVES and
OFFICERS who are making sense of this, they nod to each other as if to say,
"well we know what we have to do..."

NARRATOR
So Fay Barringer was charged with the murder of her son and Sydney Barringer noted
as an accomplice in his own death...
CAMERA moves towards the little EIGHT YEAR OLD BOY as he watches the older
couple CRY and SCREAM as detectives begin to cuff them --

NARRATOR
...and it is in the humble opinion of this narrator that this is not just "Something
That Happened." This cannot be "One of those things..." This, please, cannot be that.
And for what I would like to say, I can't.
This Was Not Just A Matter Of Chance.
CAMERA pushes in towards the MOTHER as she screams and screams and the
officer's fight to regain control of her -- in the scuffle, the apartment door is shut directly
in the face of the CAMERA.

CUT TO BLACK.
NARRATOR
Ohhhh. These strange things happen all the time.
Main title que begins, then carries over following until noted:
Title Card: New Line Cinema presents
Title Card: a Joanne Sellar/Ghoulardi Film Company Production
Title Card: a P.T. Anderson picture

CUT TO:
CAMERA DOLLIES IN Super Quick on a flower.(time lapse,bud blooms)
Freeze Frame, continue w/optical Zoom and rotate 360 degrees;total blur.
Flash title card:
M a g n o l i a
CAMERA keeps moving in further and farther until the image gets incredibly blurry,
then:

CUT TO:
INT. SUBURBAN HOME - DAY (Present Day, 1998) Sequence A
CAMERA DOLLIES IN QUICK towards a TELEVISION in a living room. It is
playing an infomercial, shot on video with a hot shot guy FRANK T.J. MACKEY (30s)
looking into the LENS.

FRANK
In this big game that we play it is not what you find and it's not what you deserve - It's
What You Take.

I'm Frank T.J. Mackey, Master of the Muffin and author of the Seduce and Destroy System of audio and videocassettes that will teach you the techniques to have any hard-body blonde dripping to wet your dock!

CAMERA moves INTO THE TELEVISION, QUICK DISSOLVE TO:

INT. BAR SET/LOCATION - THAT MOMENT

We are in the video (paneled 1.33) sales pitch/infomercial.

Various settings: The bar, a supermarket, a bedroom, a parked car.

Each has a few semi-geeks talking to a bunch of sexy young girls.

FRANK (contd.)

Bottom line? Language. The magical key to unlocking any woman's analytical ability and tap directly into her hopes, wants, fears, desires and panties.

"Seduce and Destroy," creates an immediate sexual attraction in any muffin you meet. Learn how to make that lady - "friend" your sex-starving-servant. Create an instant, money-back guaranteed trance-like state that'll have any little so and so just begging for it.

I don't care about how you look, what car you drive or what your last bank statement says: "Seduce and Destroy," is gonna teach you how to get that naughty sauce you want - fast!

(dramatic stop, then:)

Hey -- how many more times do you need to here the all too famous line of:

"I just don't feel that way about you."

CUT TO:

INT. SMILING PEANUT BAR - NIGHT

CAMERA moves in on a young woman CLAUDIA (20s) sitting alone, bit drunk.

A vaguely creepy looking MIDDLE AGED GUY (40s) takes a seat next to her:

MIDDLE AGED GUY

Hey.

CLAUDIA

Hi.

CUT TO:

INT. CLAUDIA'S APARTMENT - LATER

A series of quick shots where the following happens; CLAUDIA and the MIDDLE AGED GUY stumble into her apartment. CAMERA DOLLIES in quick as she ~norts a line of coke from her coffee table....TILT up and PAN over to him....

MIDDLE AGED GUY

So?

CUT TO:

INT. CLAUDIA'S BEDROOM - MOMENTS LATER

CAMERA DOLLIES in quick as they're having sex. He's on top of her, she's below, CAMERA lands in a CLOSE UP of her face as she gets through the experience...CAMERA moves up and past her, finds the reflection of the TELEVISON in a picture frame on her wall....

DISSOLVE TO:
INT. TELEVISION IMAGE - CLIP - THAT MOMENT
This is a promo for a game show called, "WHAT DO KIDS KNOW?" featuring the host JIMMY GATOR (60s) We see various clips of him over the years, hosting the show, at various clebrity events, etc. (Director's Note)

PROMO ANNOUNCER
For over thirty years, America has hung out and answered questions with Jimmy Gator. An American Legend and a true television icon,
Jimmy celebrates his 200,000th hour of broadcast this week --
CLIP OF JIMMY speaking to an INTERVIEWER.

JIMMY
God, have I been around that long?
INT. JIMMY GATOR'S OFFICE - DAY
Blind's closed, door locked. Jimmy and a YOUNG SHOWGIRL from some other show are having sex on his couch. CAMERA DOLLIES IN FAST.

PROMO ANNOUNCER
He's a family man who's been married for over forty years -- with two children and one grandchild on the way --
CU. PHOTOGRAPH.
A family photo of JIMMY, his wife ROSE, his son JIM, JR. and CLAUDIA.
This photo is circa 1987. OPTICAL ZOOM INTO photo that isolates Jimmy and Claudia in the picture.

CUT TO:
INT. CEDARS SINAI MEDICAL CENTER - HALLWAY - PRESENT DAY
JIMMY and ROSE (50s) walk down a hallway towards a door.
PROMO ANNOUNCER (contd.)
We've tuned in each day to see the human interaction between Jimmy and some very special kids over the years --

CUT TO:
INT. DOCTOR'S OFFICE - MOMENTS LATER
CAMERA pushes in on JIMMY and ROSE as they enter, WHIPS over to a NURSE who looks up, smiles says "hello."
PROMO ANNOUNCER (contd.)
-- and we hope there's thirty more years of watching that happen.
JIMMY (to Nurse)
...Jimmy Gator...

CUT TO:

INT. SUBURBAN HOME - DAY
CAMERA DOLLIES in towards the televison again. A quick highlight clip shows a ten year old kid named STANLEY SPECTOR answering question after question on the show, "What Do Kids Know?" in a series of dissolves;

STANLEY
...Donald W. Winnicott....1911...North America....
...South America....the answer is four....
...the answer is 22...the answer is gravity.... the answer is "The Life of Samuel Johnson."

CUT TO:
INT. SPECTOR HOUSE - DAY
CAMERA is HAND HELD and moving around a small apartment, watching a ten year old kid STANLEY SPECTOR (dressed in a suit) as he dumps dog food into two bowls for two dogs yapping around his legs while he simultaneously tries to gather his backpacks -- His father enters:
RICK SPECTOR (late 30s) starts barking directions;

RICK
Let's go,let's go, let's go, you shoulda done that ten minutes ago --

STANLEY
We need more dog food --

RICK
-- talk in the car, talk in the car, moves your ass, c'mon --
Stanley grabs two BACKPACKS and puts them over each arm. Rick grabs another bag....heads for the door....Stanley is about to fall over with these two full packs, but reaches for another bag on the floor...

RICK
Cmon,cmon,cmon, that one to?

STANLEY
I need this one.

RICK
Why the hell do you need all four bags of books to go to school each day?

STANLEY
I can't carry all of them.
I need them. I need my books.
I need them to go to school.

CUT TO:
EXT. SPECTOR HOUSE - MOMENTS LATER

CAMERA pushes in quick as Rick sits in the car, engine running, watching
Stanley struggle to get himself and the backpacks in;

RICK
There's no reason for this many backpacks.
CAMERA LANDS IN CLOSE UP of STANLEY as he slams the car door.

CUT TO:
EXT. SCHOOL - MOMENTS LATER
CAMERA PULLS BACK from the parked car in a new location as Stanley gets out of
the car with his backpacks, Rick watches from the driver's seat;

RICK
Be ready at two --

STANLEY
Should be one-thirty.

RICK
I got an audition, I won't make it here 'till two, c'mon, I'll see you later. Love you.

STANLEY
Love you too.
Rick drives off real quick. Stanley looks around at his backpacks.

CUT TO:
INT. 1960's SUBURBAN HOME - DAY
CAMERA pushes in on an old television set playing a clip from "What Do Kids Know?"
(1968) The clip shows a younger JIMMY GATOR asking questions to a ten year old
kid named DONNIE SMITH.

JIMMY
Donnie, you have an answer?

DONNIE
Promethius.

JIMMY
It is!
TELEVISION CLIP continues and we see DONNIE and two other KIDS receive a
check from the younger JIMMY GATOR in the amount of 100,000 dollars each. CU -
Young Donnie Smith as he smiles, accepts check, shakes hands with Jimmy.
TITLE CARD reads: Quiz Kid Donnie Smith - 1968

CUT TO:
INT. DENTIST OFFICE/EXAMINING ROOM - MOMENTS LATER

DONNIE SMITH, aged 40, is reclined back in a dentist chair.
He has spiky hair, a small stud earing and a bad grey suit.
TITLE CARD reads: Quiz Kid Donnie Smith - Today

DONNIE
This is really exiting....bet you don't get many people my age getting braces --
CU - Donnie opens wide and the pink gook-imprint is placed in his mouth.
CU - A Nurse holds it in there and smiles, says:

NURSE #1
You were really cute when you were on that show --

NURSE #2
-- you can't answer any questions right now though, huh? He-he-he.
CU - Teeth. The gook imprint is taken out of his mouth.

CUT TO:
INT. DENTIST OFFICE/HALLWAY - LATER
CAMERA pulls back as DONNIE and his dentist, DR. LEE (Asian, 40s) exit an
examining room, smiling, through with their appointment...

DR. LEE
So we're all set to go, Donnie.

DONNIE
Great, great, great, so I'll see you tommorrow morning.

DR. LEE
You're running around like crazy, huh?

DONNIE
I'm gonna be late for work.

CUT TO:
EXT. 7-11/PARKING LOT - NORTH HOLLYWOOD - DAY
CAMERA pushes in towards Donnie as he pulls into the parking lot in his little HONDA
ACCORD. He's smiling and singing along to a song* as he pulls into a parking space....
...but he's going just a bit too fast...and in a flash, he's over the parking stopper and up
on the curb and taps the glass store front just enough to have GLASS FALL AND
SHATTER and DISPLAYS

FALL OVER ONTO THE HOOD OF THE CAR....
CAMERA pushes in on Donnie and some people running over to see what's happend....

DONNIE
What the hell? What the hell?

PEDESTRIAN
Hey! It's Quiz Kid Donnie Smith.

PEDESTRIAN #2
Quiz Kid Donnie, why'd you drive into the seven eleven?

CUT TO:
INT. EARL'S HOUSE - DAY
CAMERA pushes in real fast on the front door as PHIL PARMA (20s) enters.
He has a flat top, flip shade sunglasses that he flips up and he's carrying 7-11 coffee and a donut....CAMERA WHIPS LFT to reveal;
In this nice house in Encino, a medical bed has been planted in the middle of the living room. In the bed is EARL PARTRIDGE (70s) He is very thin and bald and he is on his last legs, dying from cancer.
There are four or five MUTT DOGS that sleep on his lap and around the bed and at the sound of the door they are up and BARKING.
A young MEXICAN NURSE sits next to Earl, motions to Phil and his post is relieved. Phil moves in next to the bed, pets Earl's head;

PHIL
How's today then?

EARL
Fuckin' bullshit is what this is.

PHIL
Fuckin' bullshit is right, in'it?

**CAMERA MOVES INTO A CLOSE UP ON EARL, MOVES INTO HIS THROAT, QUICK
DISSOLVE INTO:**
INT. EARL'S THROAT - THAT MOMENT
CAMERA moves around his throat and through his body, looking at his BLOOD STREAM and watching, like a MEDICAL FILM, the cancer as it eats away at his body...as we see it at work we hear a WHISPER that is EARL'S VOICE:

EARL'S WHISPER VOICE
...fuckin regret, move through this life....
..and we do these things...get that back...
...forget, forget....fuck....fuck......
...make it right....and we do these things....

QUICK DISSOLVE TO:
INT. EARL'S LIVING ROOM - THAT MOMENT

CAMERA PULLS BACK from Earl's throat to his MOUTH and his EYES and he looks
to Phil says;

EARL
I'm onna need your help, Phil.
...you gotta help me something today...
CAMERA PANS over quick to PHIL.

PHIL
I'll take care of anything, Earl.
CAMERA PANS/DOLLIES away and TILTS up to the cieling;

QUICK DISSOLVE TO:
INT. EARL'S HOUSE/UPSTAIRS BEDROOM - THAT MOMENT
CAMERA dollies in on LINDA PARTRIDGE (30s) as she paces around in a
nightgown, pops a pill, talks on the phone;

LINDA
Well, you're his doctor and that's why -- well tell me something -- tell me something --
XCU, She sees the the bottle of pills she is popping from is empty.
LINDA (contd.)
And he needs more pills, then.
(beat)
Fuck it, I'm coming to see you,
I need to come see you to get him more pills and I need some answers so you better just
talk to me, I'm coming to see you, I'm coming to see you --
She SLAMS down the phone.

CUT TO:
INT. EARL'S HOUSE - LIVING ROOM - MOMENTS LATER
CAMERA moves with Linda as she comes down the stairs, walks over towards Earl's
bed, trying to hide her state. Phil stands up and looks to her.

PHIL
Hi, Linda.
EXTREME CLOSE UP 2-SHOT. Linda and Earl. He opens his eyes just a bit.
She bends in and gives him a kiss on the forehead.

LINDA
I love you, my darling.
She turns quickly, speaks as she walks out;

LINDA
I'll be back in a while, Phil.
I have to go get some things and
I have to see something and I'll be back....

She continues to talk as she walks out the door.

CUT TO:
INT. GARAGE/LINDA'S MERCEDES - PARKED - MOMENTS LATER
CAMERA DOLLIES IN real quick as she gets behind the wheel. She SMASHES her fists on the steering wheel and cries and cries and cries.

CUT TO:
INT. JIM KURRING'S APARTMENT - DAY
A very straight ahead apartment in Reseda where JIM KURRING (30s) lives.
SOUND of a 1-900 PERSONAL DATING SERVICE plays over following quick shots of Kurring getting ready for his day;
-Jim is sipping his morning coffee, reading the paper.
-Jim in the shower.
-Jim doing push ups.
-Jim watching and laughing a bit with the Today Show.
-Jim kneeling down by his bed, praying.

PHONE SERVICE VOICE
...Press One to hear this person's personal description of themself and Two to leave a a personal message of your own --
The SOUND of touch-tone phone pressing "1."

JIM KURRING'S VOICE
Well, hello. This is Jim. I work in
Law Enforcement. I am an officer for the L.A.P.D. and I work out of the Van Nuys district. I love my job, and I love to go to the movies. I try to stay pyhsically fit, my job demands it, so I'm in pretty good shape.
I'm gettin' up there, though: I'm 32 years old and I'm six feet two inches tall and I weigh about 160.
I'm really interested in meeting someone special who likes quiet things.....my life is very stressful and I'd hope to have a relationship that is very calm and undemanding and loving --
The SOUND again of the touch-tone phone cancels Jim's description.

PHONE SERVICE VOICE
If you would like to hear more personal descriptions from other men in your area, press two now --

CUT TO:
INT. VAN NUYS POLICE STATION - DAY
CAMERA observing the officers at a morning role call, DOLLIES and BOOMS DOWN towards JIM KURRING, sitting off to the side a bit by himself.

POLICE CAPTAIN (OC)

...so much violence...but that's the way of the world...good luck, as always...Serve and Protect and all that other blah-blah-blah on the side of the car it says --

CUT TO:
INT. POLICE GARAGE - MOMENTS LATER
CAMERA DOLLIES w/Jim Kurring as he walks to his squad car.
All the cops walk with partners, except him. Kurring throws on a pair of Oakley sunglasses and gets in the car --

CUT TO:
INT. POLICE CAR - MOVING - LATER
CAMERA holds a CU. of Jim as he drives. He speaks to someone unseen;

JIM KURRING
This is not an easy job. I get a call from Shirley on the radio: Bad News.
It's never good news. She tries to be cheerful, tries to say something nice, but uh-huh, it's just Bad News.
And It Stinks. But this is my job.
And I Love It. Because I want to do well.
In this life and in this world I want to do well. And I want to help people.
And I may get twenty bad calls a day.
But one time I help someone, I Make A Save?
I correct a wrong or right a situation;
Then I'm a happy cop. And We Move Through
This Life We Should Try And Do Good.
WIDER ANGLE reveals that he is talking to himself. BEAT. HOLD.
JIM KURRING (sotto, to himself)
...Do Good. And If We Can Do That...And
Not Hurt Anyone Else.....Well, Then....

CUT TO:
EXT. MAGNOLIA BOULEVARD - DAY
CAMERA looks straight down on an intersection. Jim Kurring's POLICE
CAR drives past....a little SUNLIGHT that hits the intersection goes away as if covered very quickly by a grey cloud....End Title Oue and
Sequence A.

CUT TO BLACK.
TITLE CARD reads: Partly Cloudy, 75% chance of rain

FADE IN:
INT. APARTMENT COMPLEX/NORTH HOLLYWOOD - DAY Sequence B
CAMERA (STEADICAM) follows behind JIM KURRING. He walks through a courtyard, past some young mexican and black kids playing, up a staircase and arrives at a door that is half open;

JIM KURRING
Hello?
He knocks, pushes the door open a bit, steps in: A very, very large black woman, MARCIE (4Os) appears, coming at him, ranting and raving;

MARCIE
What? What? What now?

JIM KURRING
Quietly, slow down, whoa --

MARCIE
You can't just come in here.

JIM KURRING
The door was open, I got a call --

MARCIE
You're just come in --

JIM KURRING
Calm down.

MARCIE
I am calm.

JIM KURRING
I got a call to this apartment, report of a disturbance --

MARCIE
There's no disturbance.

JIM KURRING
I got a call of a disturbance, you're door was open, I just wanna see what's goin' on --

MARCIE
There's no disturbance.

JIM KURRING
Then you've got nothin' to worry about.

MARCIE
You don't tell me, I know my rights, just come right in, you can't --

JIM KURRING

Don't test me, you wanna talk about what the law book says, we can do that, push me far enough and I'll take you to jail -- now calm down.

MARCIE
I AM CALM.
JIM KURRING
You're not calm. You're screamin' and yellin' and I'm here to check on a disturbance that was reported and that's what I'm gonna do - now are you alone in here?

MARCIE
I don't have to answer your questions.

JIM KURRING
No you don't: But I'm gonna ask you one more time: Are you alone in here?

MARCIE
What does it look like?

JIM KURRING
No one else in here?

MARCIE
You're here.

JIM KURRING
OK. That's true. Is anyone else, besides me and besides you in this house?

MARCIE
No. I said that.

JIM KURRING
Are you lyin' to me?

MARCIE
I live alone.

JIM KURRING
Maybe so, but I'm gonna ask you one more time: Is Anyone Else In This House Right Now?

MARCIE
No I Said.

JIM KURRING
Ok. What's your name?

MARCIE
Marcie.

JIM KURRING
Ok. Marice why don't you take a seat for me?

MARCIE
I preffer to stand.

JIM KURRING
I'm not askin', Marcie.
Marcie sits down.

MARCIE
I didn't do anything.

JIM KURRING
Maybe you didn't, but I'm here to find out about a disturbance.
Some neighbors called said they heard screaming and a loud crash.

MARCIE
I don't know a loud crash.

JIM KURRING
And what about screaming?

MARCIE
I said: I DON'T KNOW. You can't just come in here and start pokin' around --

JIM KURRING
What's this, how did this happen?

INSERT, ECU. THE FLOOR.
An ashtray has fallen on the floor, cigarette butts all around.

MARCIE
An ashtray fell, I don't know, maybe last night, I just woke up.

JIM KURRING
You just woke up. And what'd you have a party last night, the way this place looks?

MARCIE
I went out last night.

JIM KURRING

Ok. Marcie. Starting now I want you to have a new attitude with me. The more you play games, the more suspicious I'm gonna become that you've been up to something.

MARCIE
It's a free country, you can think anything you want.

JIM KURRING
Yes I can, Marcie. And until you start givin' me some straight answers: I'm gonna assume that some mischief has been goin' on here.

MARCIE
Mischief? What the fuck you talkin' about, mischief?

JIM KURRING
Bad and illegal behavior. That's what I mean.
Ok? Mischief. Now have you been doin' some drugs today?

MARCIE
No.

JIM KURRING
You on any medication?

MARCIE
No.

JIM KURRING
Been drinkin' today?

MARCIE
It's ten o'clock in the morning --
There's a small THUMP noise OC. Jim turns his head quick and looks and Marcie freezes.

JIM KURRING
--- What was that?

MARCIE
I didn't hear anything.
Marcie stands up.

JIM KURRING
No. No. Stay down, Marcie, sit back down on that couch --

MARCIE
I don't have to do a god damn thing.

Kurring gets his handcuffs out and handcuffs her wrist to the couch, she goes crazy, screaming and yelling the whole time;

MARCIE
WHAT'S THIS? WHAT'S THIS? GOD DAMN
BULLSHIT. BULLSHIT. DON'T PUT THOSE --
JIM KURRING
Marcie - CALM DOWN. CALM DOWN and don't do this. I want you to stay --
Continue with that until he's got her cuffed to the couch.
He removes his REVOLVER from his holster and starts to move slowly down the hall to the back bedroom --

MARCIE
WHAT THE FUCK IS THIS BULLSHIT?
WHAT THE FUCK ARE YOU DOING, MOTHERFUCKER?
MOTHER-GOD-DAMN FUCKER. WHERE ARE YOU GOIN'?
DON'T GO IN MY GOD DAMN BEDROOM.
Kurring keeps moving slowly, gun drawn, CAMERA behind him;

JIM KURRING
This is the LAPD. If anyone is back here I want you to come out and I want you to show yourself to me with your hands in the air --

MARCIE
THERE'S NO ONE IN THERE. STAY OUT
OF MY MOTHERFUCKIN BEDROOM.
Kurring moves into the BEDROOM now and sees that the CLOSET is closed and probably the only place for someone to be hiding;

JIM KURRING
This is the LAPD, if anyone is in the closet I want you to come out and show yourself to me, slowly and with your hands up --

MARCIE (OC)
THERE'S NO ONE IN THERE!
JIM KURRING
Marcie - quiet down! Now if anyone is in the closet, come out now --

MARCIE (OC)
THERE'S NO ONE IN MY MOTHERFUCKIN
CLOSET AND STAY OUT OF MY BEDROOM,
STAY OUT OF MY GOD DAMN BEDROOM.
JIM KURRING
-- do not do this -- my gun is drawn and If I Have To Open That Closet you will get shot -- Step Out Now.

Jim inches towards the closet, flips it open real quick and stands back, ready for something to jump out -- nothing.

MARCIE
I told you there was no one in there!
Jim looks down the hall at Marcie who has physically dragged the large couch handcuffed behind her;

JIM KURRING
Marcie - Do not drag that couch any further!

JIM'S POV, CAMERA DOLLIES IN SLOWLY TOWARDS THE CLOSET.
He pushes some sheets aside and burries around to reveal:
A DEAD SKINNY WHITE MAN (50s) curled up in a ball on the floor of the closet.
He'd dead and he's been covered in dirty laundry. He has a gag around his mouth.
HOLD on Jim for a moment, he panics a little and swings his REVOLVER towards Marcie:

JIM KURRING
What the hell is this Marcie?

MARCIE
THAT'S NOT MINE.
Jim swings the aim of his gun back at the dead body.

CUT TO:
INT. EARL'S HOUSE - LIVING ROOM - DAY
Earl in bed, pretty out of it, but once in a while a couple clear moments. Phil sits next to the bed, paper and coffee nearby.

EARL
...n'I dowanna do this...sit here,
I can see the things, y'know...it's gettin' there that's the cocksucker...like...I see that pen...I see it, I know it's there,
I reach out for it -- no --
He mimes the action, gets nowhere near the pen.

EARL
...no...no goddamn use.
(beat)
I have a son, y'know?

PHIL
You do?

EARL

...ah...

PHIL
Where is he?

EARL
I don't know...I mean, he's around, he's here, in town, y'know, but I don't know...he's a tough one...very....
Do you have a girlfriend, Phil?

PHIL
No.

EARL
Get a girlfriend.

PHIL
I'm trying.

EARL
And do good things with her...share the thing...all that bullshit is true, y'know...find someone and hold on all that...Where's Linda?

PHIL
She went out. She said she went out to run some errands. She'll be back.

EARL
She's a good girl. She's a little nuts, but she's a good girl I think.
She's a little daffy.

PHIL
She loves you.

EARL
...ah...maybe...yeah...she's a good one...

PHIL
When was the last time you talked to your son?

EARL
....I dunn...o....maybe ten...five, fuck, fuck....that's another thing that goes --

PHIL
-- memory?

EARL

Time lines, y'know? I remember things but not so -- right there -- y'know?

PHIL
Yeah.

EARL
"yeah." the fuck do you know?

PHIL
I've seen it before.

EARL
Other fuckin' assholes like me.

PHIL
There's no asshole like you.

EARL
...cocksucker....

PHIL
How come every word you say is either
"cocksucker," or "shitballs," or "fuck?"

EARL
Do me a personal favor --

PHIL
Go fuck myself?

EARL
You got it.
EARL gets hit with something and starts to MOAN a bit. Sharp pain hitting him and he
touches his hand to his face....

EARL
...I can't hold onto this anymore...

PHIL
I'll get you another pain pill.
Another morphine pill --

EARL
...gimme that fuckin' phone...

PHIL

Who are you gonna call?

EARL
I wanna see this...where is he, do you know?

PHIL
Who?

EARL
Jack.

PHIL
Is Jack your son?
Earl doesn't answer. He's drifting a bit more now.

PHIL
You wanna call him on the phone?
We can call him, I can dial the phone if you can remember the number --

EARL
-- it's not him. it's not him.
He's the fuckin' asshole...Phil..c'mere...
Phil leans in closer to Earl.

EARL
This is so boring...so goddamn... and dying wish and all that, old man on a bed...fuck...wants one thing:

PHIL
It's ok.
Earl hallucinates a bit, cries a little, tries to form the sentences;

EARL
...find him on the...Frank. His name's
Frank Mackey --

PHIL
Frank Mackey. That's your son?

EARL that'snotmy name...find Lily, gimmme that, give it --
Earl tries to grab something near Phil's head that is not there.
He's hallucinating more now, falls asleep a bit, mumbling;

EARL ifyougimmethat....overonthe....fuck....
I can't hold ontothis anymore...
He gives Phil make an imaginary object and falls asleep. BEAT.

Stay with Phil a moment as he turns his head, looking around the house a moment, looks back to Earl.

CUT TO:
INT. BURBANK HOLIDAY INN/BANQUET ROOM - THAT MOMENT
FRANK steps into a CLOSE UP and holding a mic, says:

FRANK
Respect the cock and tame the cunt, boys.
REVERSE, THAT MOMENT. The crowd of fifty GUYS who are taking the
"Seduce and Destroy Seminar" that Frank is teaching today laugh and play along;
Frank is on a slightly elevated stage. vBehind him a huge banner for,
"Seduce and Destroy," whose logo is a scared pussycat and a large wolf with a big buldge in his fur. It reads: "No Pussy Has Nine Lives".

FRANK
And you did hear me right. Tame it.
Take it on, head first -- with your skills at work and say, "No. You will not control me. You will not take my soul and you will not win this game."
'cause it is a game, guys, you wanna think it's not -- go back to the schoolyard and have a crush on Mary Jane -- respect the cock -- you are embedding this thought:
I'm in charge. I'm the one who says yes, no, now or here. Shit, man. Sad but true.
Sad But True. And you wanna know what?
It must be the way.
The thing about chicks and the thing about this course that we're going through today is how universal the whole thing is. I mean: I wish I could sit here and say that it's not -- because the reality?
If each chick had something new, something really new that I'd never seen before?
Fuckin' hell: I'd be in the money! Because
I'd have to create a hundred new cassettes, a hundred new books, a hundred new seminars and hundred new videos just to deal with each and every situation a chick could create - but that is just not the case. They are universal.
They are sheep. They are to be studied and watched -- they have patterns that must be stopped, interupted and resisted. I'd be makin' a fuckin' butt load if they were actually as much of a challenge as they want you to think they are!
Reality: They Are All The Same.
Each and every one of them. And once you learn these methods: You're Set. You Don't Have To Come Back.
That's it. In solid. Boom. Done. Over. Why?
Because all women are the same. Period.
End of discussion. Sorry. It's true. Sad But True.
And anyone who wants to say that these methods we work by are "unfair?" Yes, they are.
Guilty as charged. And so's the world.
It's a harsh, hard unfair place, but it's not gonna stop me from getting my fair shair of hair pie --

Period. Sorry. End of discussion.

CUT TO:
INT. HOLIDAY INN/LOBBY - THAT MOMENT
Sliding doors open in the lobby and a young woman GWENOVIER (30s) enters, takes off her sunglasses and looks around.
There's a bunch of Posters and Signs for the "Seduce and Destroy
Seminar with Frank TJ Mackey," etc. Frank's two sidekicks: DOC (20s) and CAPTAIN MUFFY (40s) approach;

CAPTAIN MUFFY
You're Gwenovier?

GWENOVIER
Yeah.

CAPTIAN MUFFY
I'm Captain Muffy, I'm Frank's personal assistant. This is Doc --

DOC
Hello.

GWENOVIER
Hello.

CAPTAIN MUFFY
We can go right in here. He started about thirty five minutes ago, but it's all getting pumped up now --

CUT TO:
INT. HOLIDAY INN/BANQUET ROOM - THAT MOMENT
Captain Muffy, Doc and Gwenovier enter and head tor some seats,
CAMERA swings a 180 and moves down the aisle, towards the stage as Frank speaks
--

FRANK
Number One: Get a calendar. I cannot stress this enough. This is a simple item guys. It's 99 cents at your corner store: Go And Get One. Fuck it, if you reach into your packet, you'll see I've been nice enough to include one, 'cause that's the kind of prick I am --
You're gonna need this calendar and I know it sounds like a small thing, but having it makes all the difference in the world:
If you meet a girl and you're gonna work an A-3 Interuption -- let's say an eight day waiting period before the next call -- how you gonna know when those eight days are up? Buy a calendar.
Next move? Mark the calendar.

Yeah, yeah, yeah. What did I pay my eight hundred dollars for? To hear Frank tell me to buy a calendar and mark it? Just stick with me and stick by the calendar. Mark it up -- use it to set goals -- If you wanna make that "friend" something else -- you gotta be hard on yourself, set goals:
(beat, to audience)
You, there: And What's Your Name?

CUT TO:
INT. EARL'S HOUSE/OFFICE - THAT MOMENT
Phil flips through a little adress book, finds a number. XCU - It reads,
"Frank 8/509-9027" He picks up a phone and dials;

FEMALE VOICE
Hello?

PHIL
Hi. Is Frank there?

FEMALE VOICE
I think you have the wrong number.

PHIL
I'm looking for Frank Mackey.

FEMALE VOICE
No.

PHIL
Is this 509-9027?

FEMALE VOICE
Yeah. You have the wrong number.
There's no one named Frank here.

PHIL
Alright. Thank you.

FEMALE VOICE
Yep.
Phil hangs up the phone.

CUT TO:
INT. HOLIDAY INN/BANOUET ROOM - THAT MOMENT.
CAMERA with Gwenovier as she walks quietly over to the side of the crowd to a VIDEO CREW that's been set up and is recording
Frank's seminar. She speaks sotto to a CAMERAMAN;

GWENOVIER
Sorry I'm late --

CAMERAMAN
-- we're all set upstairs.

GWENOVIER
Thanks.
She moves towards a row and takes a seat next to Captain Muffy and Doc, speaks sotto
again;

DOC
You have everything you need?

GWENOVIER
I'm set, thanks.
CAMERA moves away, Frank is kneeling down to a GUY in the audience, interacting,
speaking compassionately;

FRANK
Denise?

GUY
That's right --

FRANK
-- and she hurt you didn't she?
I know, I know. I know how that can be brother, but let me tell you loud and clear what
we will be teaching
Denise when we put our calendars to work and set goals:
Frank hops back up on the stage;

FRANK
Little Denise, I say this: I mark it up and I write it down and you've been warned:
"By the end of May, you will know I'm not gay."
"On the fourth of June, Denise, you're gonna be lickin' my spoon."
"And Come August, You Suck My Big Fat
Sausage." I've SET GOALS FOR MYSELF.
And what? I've said "enough is enough."
Because why? She's not gonna be your pal.
She's not gonna be your friend. You think she's gonna be there for you the second you
need something? Think again - this fuckin' bitch Denise!
(audience cheers)

But: Listen up: That is not to say that we don't all need women as friends, 'cause we're gonna learn later on in Chapter 23 that having a couple of chick-friends laying around can come in real handy in setting Jealousy Traps.

But we'll get to that. Number One (this is page 18 in your booklets, blue cover - go to it and follow along with me.)

The guys flip open their little blue booklets and follow along.

FRANK
Create a crisis -- simple and clean, and if done properly can be quite effective in getting some bush.
Here we go: Set a date with your so-called
"friend." Let's say you make it 7:30.
You call her on the phone --

FLASH ON:
INT. GIRL'S APARTMENT - NIGHT
CAMERA DOLLIES AROUND a young GIRL (20s) on the phone.

GIRL
That sounds like fun, Frank.
I love seafood.

CUT TO:
INT. FRANK'S APARTMENT - NIGHT
Frank on the phone.

FRANK
So I'll see you about 7:30?
Great, then. Bye-bye, Cindy.
He hangs up.

CUT TO:
INT. GIRL'S HOUSE - ANOTHER NIGHT
CAMERA (HAND HELD) follows behind the GIRL as she walks from the kitchen to the front door, shaking her head, huffing and puffing....

FRANK (VO)
You wait until about nine o'clock and you ring the doorbell.
She opens the door and sees FRANK, crying and hysterical.

FRANK (VO)
She opens it up, pissed as hell, but finds you sobbing your eyes out --
Frank looks up at her and says:

FRANK
...I can't believe what happened...

Frank and the Girl sit down on the couch together.

FRANK (VO)
You explain between sobs that you hit a dog on the way over to pick her up and you had to rush it to the animal hospital but by the time you got there --

FRANK
...and it's paw was sticking out... and it was too late. It was too late.
She moves in and hugs him.

GIRL
Ohhh, shhhh...shhh...Frank...

CUT TO:
INT. HOLIDAY INN/BANQUET ROOM - THAT MOMENT
Frank is cracking himself up. He continues.

FRANK
I can't believe I'm telling you guys this, but the truly terrifying part is that: THIS WORKS.
Any girl that calls herself your friend is not gonna let you be alone in a situation like that.
Technique #2: Staging a fight.
This is not knock down, drag out, crying screaming, yelling -- this is a simple, direct and subtle way of planting confusion into a girl's mind. Remember we are using reinforcement technique "G" with these women.
Here's how:

CUT TO:
INT. GIRL'S HOUSE - NIGHT
The Girl picks up her phone and presses some numbers...

FRANK (VO)
One day, she calls you up on the phone...

CUT TO:
INT. FRANK'S HOUSE - NIGHT
Frank picks up the phone.

FRANK
Hello?

GIRL
Hey, Frank. It's Cindy. I'm wondering if you wanna grab a bite and see a movie?

FRANK (VO)

You very directly say:

FRANK
"I don't think I have anything to say to you, Cindy."
Frank hangs up the phone.

CUT TO:
INT. GIRL'S HOUSE - THAT MOMENT
The Girl gets the dial tone. She looks completely confused and hurt.

CUT TO:
INT. HOLIDAY INN/BANQUET ROOM - BACK TO SCENE
Frank speaking to the group:

FRANK
Let her wonder what she did wrong.
CAMERA DOES A SLOW DOLLY IN. Frank's tone changes a bit, gets darker:

FRANK
This is the way...because they will always wonder, "What did I do?"
"What could I have done different?"
"How should I behave to get this back?"
And if they think that way -- then they are asking for you to hurt them and
That Is What You Must Do. That is what you must do which is punish them many,
many times over.

CUT TO:
INT. CEDARS SINAI MEDICAL CENTER - HALLWAY - DAY
CAMERA pushes in as LINDA walks towards us, down the same hallway we saw
Jimmy Gator walking down earlier, she heads into an office --

CUT TO:
INT. DOCTOR'S OFFICE/RECPETION AREA - MOMENTS LATER
CAMERA pushes in on Linda as she enters, WHIPS over to a
RECEPTIONIST who looks up;

RECEPTIONIST
Mrs. Partridge --

LINDA
I'm here and I need to see him.

CUT TO:
INT. DOCTOR'S OFFICE - MOMENTS LATER
Quick shots get them in the room: DR. LANDON (40s) sits across from LINDA, who's
in semi-hysterics, pacing;

LINDA
-- he's fucking dying, he's dying as we're sitting here and there isn't a fucking thing -- jesus, how can you tell me to calm down?

DR. LANDON
I can help you through this the best I know how but there are certain things you are gonna have to be strong about and take care of, now we can go over them, but I need to know that you're listening to me, ok?

LINDA
I just, I just -- I just -- I'm just in a fucking state, I know he's going and it's like I don't know how
-- just tell me practical things --
What the fuck do I do with his body?
What happens when he dies? That next moment:
What? What do I do? Then What?

DR. LANDON
Well that's what Hospice will take care of for you. They will send a nurse, someone who can take care of all of that for you --

LINDA
He has Phil right now.

DR. LANDON
Phil's one of the nurses from the service?

LINDA
Yeah.

DR. LANDON
If you're happy with Phil taking care of him and helping you, that's fine, but contact Hospice to arrange for the body --

LINDA
-- you don't understand: it's more pain than before and the fucking morphine pills aren't working, he's -- past two days it's like he can't really swallow them and I don't know if they're going down -- I can't see inside his mouth anymore -- I'm up all night staring at him and I don't think the pills are going down and he moans and he hurts --

DR. LANDON
We can fix that, because I can give you -- are you listening?

LINDA
I'm listening. I'm getting better.

DR. LANDON
Do you wanna sit down?

LINDA
I need to sit down.

DR. LANDON
Ok. Linda: Earl is not gonna make it.
He's dying. He is. He is dying very, very rapidly --
She breaks a bit more.

DR. LANDON
Now the thing here is making that experience as painless and easy as possible for him,
you understand? Now you need to get in touch with Hospice care because they can take
care of all those practical things that you're asking me about -- they are who you call
when he dies.
He writes a number on his bussiness card, hands it over as they speak;

DR. LANDON
This is the number for Hospice.
Ok. Now. As far as the morphine pills go, there is something else to consider that can
take the pain away that he is in, there is a very strong and very potent solution of liquid
morphine....it's a little bottle, with an eye dropper and it's easy to get in his mouth and
drop on his tounge and it will certainly diminish the pain that he is in but you have to
realize that once you give it to him; there really is no coming back, I mean, it will
certainly cure his pain, but he will float in and out of consciousness, even worse than
he is now, Linda. I mean, any sign of the recognizable Earl will pretty much go away -
-

LINDA
-- how the fuck can I say anything to that -- I don't know what to say to that --

DR. LANDON
The job here is to make him as comfortable as possible -- right now -- our job is to just
try and make it as painless as possible.
Right? You understand?
CAMERA pushes into an EXTREME CLOSE UP on Dr. Landon's hands writing the
perscription for the liquid morphine....hands it to Linda....

CUT TO:
INT. JIMMY'S JAGUAR - PARKED - DAY
CAMERA holds a CU on Jimmy sitting behind the wheel. He hesitates a moment, exits
the car.

CUT TO:

EXT. CLAUDIA'S APARTMENT/STAIRWELL - MOMENTS LATER
CAMERA holds looking down a staircase. Jimmy enters FRAME, walks up to the second floor, stands a moment, then knocks.

CUT TO:
INT. CLAUDIA'S BEDROOM - THAT MOMENT
CAMERA DOLLIES in on the bed. Claudia's asleep. The MIDDLE AGED GUY is lying next to her in his underwear. He hears the door, wakes.

CUT TO:
EXT./INT. CLAUDIA'S APARTMENT - THAT MOMENT
Jimmy knocks again....after a BEAT...the door is opened by the MIDDLE AGED GUY. He stands in his underwear.

MIDDLE AGED GUY
Hello?

JIMMY
Hello. Is Claudia here?

MIDDLE AGED GUY
She's asleep.

BEAT.
JIMMY
Are you her boyfriend?

MIDDLE AGED GUY
You're Jimmy Gator, right?

JIMMY
Yes. What's your name?

MIDDLE AGED GUY
I'm Bob.

JIMMY
You're her boyfriend?

MIDDLE AGED GUY
No, I'm just a friend. What are you doing here, I mean...you know Claudia?

JIMMY
I'm her father.
The Middle Aged Guy looks a bit confused.

JIMMY
Can I come in?

MIDDLE AGED GUY
Yeah. She's sleeping now, I mean --
Jimmy steps inside, looks around the place, sees the coke and some pot and pills sitting
out on the coffee table.

MIDDLE AGED GUY
Want me to wake her up?

JIMMY
I'II go....is it...back here?
The Middle Aged Guy points Jimmy to the back bedroom.
INT. CLAUDIA'S BEDROOM - THAT MOMENT
Claudia is asleep. Jimmy enters, stands near the edge of the bed.
After a moment, Claudia's eyes open, look over and see Jimmy.

CLAUDIA
...what the fuck is this...?

JIMMY
It's me. Claudia. It's me.
She sits up a bit, covers herself, looks past him and sees the
Middle Aged Guy, sitting in his underwear in the living room, watching them. She looks
back to Jimmy;

CLAUDIA
What do you want? Why are you here?

JIMMY
I'd like to talk to you. Your boyfriend let me in, I just knocked on the door --

CLAUDIA
He's not my boyfriend.
Jimmy hesitates a beat, then:

CLAUDIA
Wanna call me a slut now, something?

JIMMY
No. No.
She starts to move towards tears, nervousness;

CLAUDIA
What the fuck do you want?

JIMMY
I want to sit. I want to talk to you.

CLAUDIA
Don't sit down.

JIMMY
...I want to....I want so many things, Claudia.
Maybe we can just talk to straighten our things out....there are so many things that I
want to tell you --

CLAUDIA
I don't wanna talk to you.

JIMMY
Please. It doesn't have to be now.
Maybe we can make a date to sit down,
I didn't mean to walk in on you like this --

CLAUDIA
Why are you here, why are you doing this?
Coming in here -- you wanna call me a whore?

JIMMY
I don't want you to think that I'm that way to you -- I'm not gonna call you a slut or
something --

CLAUDIA
Yeah, yeah right -- what the fuck are doing? WHAT THE FUCK ARE YOU DOING
IN MY HOUSE?

JIMMY
Don't yell, honey. Please don't go crazy --

CLAUDIA
I'M NOT CRAZY. Don't you tell me I'm crazy.

JIMMY
I'm not saying that, I'm sorry --

CLAUDIA
I'M NOT CRAZY. You're the one. You're the one who's wrong. You're the one --

JIMMY
I have something, so much -- I'm sick, Claudia.

I'm sick.

CLAUDIA
Get out of here, get the fuck out of my house --

JIMMY
Now STOP IT and LISTEN to me right now.
I AM DYING, I GOT SICK...now I fell down and I'm Not...DON'T --

CLAUDIA
GET THE FUCK OUT.
JIMMY
I'm dying, Claudia. I have cancer.
I have cancer and I'm dying, soon.
It's metastasized in my bones and I --

CLAUDIA
FUCK YOU. FUCK YOU, YOU GET OUT.
JIMMY
I'm not lying to you, I'm not --

CLAUDIA
FUCK YOU. YOU GET THE FUCK OUT OF HERE.
JIMMY baby, please, please --

CLAUDIA
I'M NOT YOUR BABY, I'M NOT YOUR GIRL.
I'm not your fuckin' baby --
She moves up in the bed, exposes a bit of her breast, tries to cover herself --

JIMMY
Please put your clothes on, please --

CLAUDIA
YOU BURN IN BELL. You burn in hell and you deserve it -- YOU GET THE FUCK
OUT.

JIMMY
Honey.

CLAUDIA
GET OUT.
BEAT. He stands a moment.

JIMMY
Your mother wants to hear from you --

CLAUDIA
GET THE FUCK OUT OF HERE.
He walks out of the bedroom, past the MIDDLE AGED GUY, who's sitting on the couch.

JIMMY
I'm sorry.

MIDDLE AGED GUY
It's alright.
Jimmy exits. Claudia is shaking and crying and holding herself in the covers of the bed.
The Middle Aged Guy snorts a line of coke, looks into her;

CLAUDIA
Can you get your shit and leave, please?

CUT TO:
INT. SOLOMON AND SOLOMON ELECTRONICS - DAY
CAMERA pushes in as Donnie Smith runs in the door, brushes his hair back, etc. This is a "Good Guys" type electronics place.
He rushes towards the back.

ANGLE, DOOR TO BACK ROOM.
CAMERA pushes in real quick and tilts down as Donnie reaches to his belt and his KEY HOLDER (one of those attached to string on the belt) He inserts the KEY.

CUT TO:
INT. BACK HALLWAY - SOLOMON AND SOLOMON - THAT MOMENT
Donnie enters, walks swiftly down the hall to another door.
Just before he reaches it, AVI SOLOMON (30s) appears at the end of the hall.

AVI
Don.
Donnie stops short, looks. Avi gives him the "follow me" finger.

DON
Hey, Avi. I'll be right there.
Avi goes back in the room he came from. Donnie does the
KEY and CODE thing now on this door.

CUT TO:
INT. DRESSING ROOM/EMPLOYEE LOUNGE - MOMENTS LATER
Donnie is changed into his Solomon and Solomon Electronics vest and name tag. He brushes himself up, sweating a bit. (Note:ON HIS BACK)

DONNIE
This is going to be ok. This is. This is.

CUT TO:
INT. SOLOMON'S OFFICE - MOMENTS LATER
Donnie sitting across the desk from SOLOMON SOLOMON (40s) owner of the store.
Avi, his brother, stands nearby.

DONNIE
...please...

SOLOMON
Don't Donnie. Don't do it.
Donnie swells up a bit, about to cry.

DONNIE
This is so fucked, Solomon.
I don't deserve this.

SOLOMON
Don't get strong, Donnie. This is making sense, this making a lot of sense.
You are not doing the job, the job
I ask you to do, a job I give you.
Over and over and over and I'm sorry.
But I'm not gonna say I'm sorry that much more.

DONNIE
Solomon: I am in the middle of so much.
So much in my life and this is --
If you do this, if you fire me: I Am Fucked.
I can't really explain much, but please, please, I've worked here for four years, four years
I've given you and I'm, I'm,
I mean what? I'm sorry I was late.
I had a car accident. I accidentaly drove into a seven-eleven. It was not my fault.

AVI
Who's fault was it, Don?

SOLOMON
Avi, please, shut the fuck up for one second. Don, how much further do you want me
to go in showing you, showing you what I've done for you in four years and what you've
done back? Do you want me to do it? I can.
The loans I've given, how much your sales are, how late you are, over and over, loosing
the keys to the Covina store --

DONNIE

I don't have any money, Solomon.
If you fire me --

SOLOMON
-- I give you money, I give you a paycheck.
Your sales suck, Don. I give, I give.
When I find you, when I meet you, what? I put you on the billboard,
I put you in the store, my salesman, my fucking representation of Solomon and Solomon
Electronic, Quiz Kid Donnie Smith from the game show --

DONNIE
I lent my name, my celebrity. Exactly --

SOLOMON
FUCK YOU. I pay you, I paid you.
I give you a fucking chance and a chance and over and over, over you let me down. I
trust you with so much.
The keys to my store, the codes to my locks, the life, the blood of my bussiness and
return is smashing in seven-eleven, late, always late, loans -- I loaned you money for
your kitchen that you never did --

DONNIE
I paid you back.

SOLOMON
Two years! Two years later and out of your paycheck, I never charge interest --

DONNIE
Solomon, please. Please. I am so fucked here if you do this. This is the worst timing.
The worst timing I could ever imagine.
I need to keep working. I have so many debts, so many things, I have, I have,
I have -- I have surgery -- I have my oral surgery coming --

AVI
What surery?

DONNIE
Oral surgery. Corrective teeth surgery.

SOLOMON
What is that?

DONNIE
Braces.

SOLOMON

Braces?

DONNIE
Yes.

SOLOMON
You don't need braces.

DONNIE
Yes I do.

SOLOMON
Your teeth are fine.

AVI
Your teeth are straight.

DONNIE
I need corrective oral surgery.
I need the braces.

AVI
Don, you got hit by lightning that time in Tahoe, you went on vacation,
I don't think braces is a good idea --

DONNIE
I can't believe you're gonna do this to me, the situation I'm in, I don't --
Avi: You know what? Being hit by lighting doesn't matter for getting braces, ok?
Now Solomon, let me just ask you once:
Please. Please. Don't do this.

AVI
How are you paying tor the braces, Donnie?

DONNIE
I don't know.

SOLOMON
And how much is braces?

DONNIE
It's...doesn't matter....

AVI
It's like five thousand dollars,
I've seen it, I know --

SOLOMON
You're pissing me off, Don. This is so unbelievable -- so fucking stupid, you're gonna
spend five thousand dollars on braces you don't need --

DONNIE
I've been a good worker --

SOLOMON
Don't do this, Don.

AVI
No need for braces, Donnie.

SOLOMON
Where are you getting the money for this?

DONNIE
I don't know.

SOLOMON
You were gonna ask me weren't you?

DONNIE
I've been a good worker, Solomon.
A hard and loyal --

AVI
No need for braces, Donnie.

DONNIE
THAT'S NONE OF YOUR BUSSINESS.
I HAVE BEEN A GOOD WORKER, A GOOD AND
LOYAL WORKER FOR YOU, YOU FUCKING ASSHOLE.
AVI
HEY FUCK YOU DON WATCH IT NOW.
SOLOMON
Give me your keys, Don.

DONNIE
PLEASE DON'T DO THIS!
SOLOMON
GIMME YOUR FUCKIN' KEYS.
BEAT. Donnie tries to calm himself, hold back tears, stands up.
He struggles with his KEY CHAIN and finally after a bunch of moments, hands over
six or seven keys.

CU. INSERT, KEYS. placed on the desk.

CUT TO:
INT. APARTMENT COMPLEX/NORTH HOLLYWOOD - THAT MOMENT
CAMERA hangs inside bedroom w/Detectives and Investigators and
County Coroner folks as we go through in a series of quick shots.
(Director's Note: very technical here. Snapshots, ECU's on body, procedure, etc.) * See
County Coroner videotape.

IN THE LIVING ROOM
CAMERA pushes in past DETECTIVES and OFFICERS who are exchanging
information...CAMERA moves towards Jim Kurring, standing off a bit now, usless to
the investigation as far as everyone else is concerned, but listening carefully to what
they say:

OFFICER
Identified as Porter Parker, aged 59.
Better known as the dead guy in the closet.
So says the building guy, this is her husband --

DETECTIVE #2
-- he's doesn't live here, but he comes around, raises shit, screaming, yelling, something
or other --

OFFICER
There's a son, apparently. And a kid.

DETECTIVE #1
Her son?

OFFICER
Her son, that's right...and the kid.
And they were here and around and from late last night and through the morning, it's
screaming and yelling --

DETECTIVE #1
And Where Are They?

DETECTIVE
-- they are not to be found.

CORONER WOMAN
-- she's got six hundred dollars and a large box of condoms next to the bed --

OFFICER #1
And three wedding rings.

DETECTIVE #1
Ok.

CORONER WOMAN
-- guys come in, out and around all day, this is the building guy talking --

OFFICER
The building guy says The Son and The
Closet guy are always goin' at it --

CORONER WOMAN
That's right.

DETECTIVE #1
And what is she saying?

OFFICER
Not a god damn thing.
CAMERA lands CU on Jim Kurring.

ANGLE, COURTYARD AREA - THAT MOMENT
Another set of Detectives/Officers/Investigators are standing over Marcie, who sits handcuffed. She has her best, "I'm not saying anything" face on. Again, they're OC througout;

OFFICER #2
Why did you kill him, Marcie?

DETECTIVE #3
Did you kill him?

OFFICER #2
Did he hurt you, did he do something?

DETECTIVE #4
How long's he been in there?

DETECTIVE #3
You're hurting yourself, Marcie.

OFFICER #3
You have the dead body of your husband in the closet of your apartment, Marcie.

OFFICER #2
That Is Not Good.

DETECTIVE #3
You hit him with the ashtray, you strangled him --

DETECTIVE #4
-- tell us he fell and hit his head, but tell us something, Marcie.

OFFICER #2
Why did you kill him?
The Main Detective from previous steps into FRAME, says:

DETECTIVE #1
-- Marcie: Where's your son? Marcie?
Marcie? Marcie tell us where your Son is now.
Marcie tell us where your son is.
CAMERA arrives CU on Marcie.

MARCIE
I wanna talk to my motherfuckin' lawyer.

ANGLE, STREET OUTSIDE APARTMENT COMPLEX - LATER
The investigation is wrapping up now and CAMERA (STEADICAM) moves with Jim
Kurring as he heads towards his squad car, talking into his WALKIE TALKIE. (Dir.
Note: technical info re: disturbance at adress/Jim takes call/etc.)

WALKIE VOICE
...4277 Tujunga...

JIM KURRING
10-4.
Out of the group of neighborhood lookie-lo's comes a little black kid who starts walking
alongside Jim Kurring as they head away from the scene -- this is DIXON, age 10. He's
very small for his age and he carries one of those boxes filled with Candy Bars he's
trying to sell. They walk/talk;

DIXON
How much you pay me for my help?

JIM KURRING
I think it's more complicated than that little man.

DIXON
Put me on the payroll, find out, find out wassup --

JIM KURRING
You don't just sign up to be a police officer -- it's about three years of training -- ok?

DIXON
I'm trained, I'm ready to go, you wanna buy some candy to help underprivelaged youth in the --

JIM KURRING
Sorry, little man.

DIXON
You wanna take my statement, I'll perform for you, gotta get paid though, gotta get PAID.

JIM KURRING
Why the hell aren't you in school?

DIXON
No school today. My teacher got sick.

JIM KURRING
They don't have substitute teachers where you go to school?

DIXON
Nope. So what'd they find out in there?

JIM KURRING
That's confidential information, little man.

DIXON
Tell me what you know, I'll tell you what I know --

JIM KURRING
No Can Do.

DIXON
Leave this one to the detectives, they ain't gonna solve shit, I can help you, make you the man with a plan, give you the gift that I flow -- think fast -- you wanna know who killed that guy?
Jim Kurring stops at his Squad Car, turns to Dixon;

JIM KURRING
Ok. Listen. You: c'mere.

DIXON
No.

JIM KURRING

You wanna disrespect an officer of the law?

DIXON
I can help you solve the case,
I can tell you who did it.

JIM KURRING
Are you a joker? huh? Tellin' jokes?

DIXON
I'm a rapper.

JIM KURRING
Oh, you're a rapper, huh? You got a record contract?

DIXON
Not yet -- "give you the clue for the bust if you show me some trust --"

JIM KURRING
Have you ever been to Juvenille Hall?

DIXON
I ain't fuckin with you --

JIM KURRING
Hey. Watch the mouth. Watch it.

DIXON
C'mon, man, just watch me, watch and listen --

JIM KURRING
Go. Hurry up. Let's go.
Dixon places his box of candy down and starts dancing around.
Jim Kurring stands beside his squad car.

DIXON
Presence - with a double ass meaning gifts I bestow, with my riff, and my flow but you
don't hear me though think fast, catch me, yo cause I throw what I know with a
Resonance - fo'yo'trouble-ass fiend in weenin yo-self off the back of the shelf
Jackass crackas, bodystackas dicktootin niggas, masturbatin' yo trigga butcha y'all just
fake-ass niggas --

JIM KURRING
-- watch the mouth, homeboy, I don't need to hear that word --

DIXON

-- livin' to get older with a chip on your shoulder
'cept you think you got a grip, cauze you hip gotta holster?
Ain't no confessor, so busta, you best just
Shut The fuck up, try to listen and learn --

JIM KURRING
Alright, alright, cut it, coolio.
That's enough with the mouth and the language.

DIXON
I'm almost done.

JIM KURRING
Finish it up without the lip.

DIXON
Check that ego - come off it -
I'm the profit - the proffesor
Ima teach you 'bout The Worm, who eventually turned to catch wreck with the neck of
a long time oppressor
And he's runnin from the devil, but the debt is always gaining
And if he's worth being hurt, he's worth bringin' pain in -
When the sunshine don't work, the Good Lord bring the rain in.

HOLD ON KURRING.
DIXON
Now that shit will help you SOLVE the case.

JIM KURRING
Whatever that meant, I'm sure it's real helpful Ice-T.
Kurring gets behind the wheel, Dixon hustles over;

DIXON
Did you listen to me?

JIM KURRING
I was listening --

DIXON
-- I told you who did it and you're not listening to me.

JIM KURRING
-- and I'm through playin' games.
Kurring closes his door and drives off...(Director's Note: Reference notes for SOUND
design here, carries over cut...)

CUT TO:
MUSIC QUE starts, builds over the following cut and through sequence;
INT. SCHOOL LIBRARY - DAY Sequence C
CAMERA PUSHES IN SLOW on STANLEY as he sits at a desk...piles of books spread out in front of him....

OVERHEAD ANGLE, LOOKING STRAIGHT DOWN ONTO:
All the books he has in front of him, we catch glimpses of things:
"How Things Work" "Forensic Studies" "The Guiness Book of World Records" "The Natural History of Nonsense" "Weather" "Learned Pigs..."
INSERT, CU. IMAGES of the book about weather. CAMERA scans, dissolves and moves around various images of ancient BAROMETERS, HYGROMETERS from the 1700's. We see 16th Century French comic strips regarding weather as cartoon characters. Aristotle pointing to the sky.
Scan past the words, "...our quest to understand and predict the weather reaches back to the Stone Age..."
CU - Stanley's face as he reads. SLOW ZOOM IN.
CU - School Bell RINGS.
CU - He grabs his books.

CUT TO:
EXT. SCHOOL - PICK UP AREA - MOMENTS LATER
CAMERA (STEADICAM) follows behind Stanley as he heads, with all his backpacks, towards Rick, who's waiting in the car --

RICK
C'mon, man.

STANLEY
You're late, not me.

RICK
You coulda been in front --

STANLEY
-- I didn't see you from the window.
Rick helps him get the bags in the car. CAMERA stays real TIGHT following STANLEY'S FACE....he sits in the car....OC we hear Rick getting in the driver's seat and starting the enqine...little droplets of RAIN start to fall on the windshield....

RICK (OC)
You ready to keep winning?

STANLEY
Sure.
STANLEY is driven away, OUT OF FRAME.

CUT TO:
EXT. SKY - DAY
CAMERA looking straight up. It starts POURING RAIN real hard right INTO CAMERA....SLOW ZOOM IN....hold until it's just a

WASH OF WATER.
Title Card reads: Temperature/Percipitation reading/ wind direction/weather info/humidity/etc

QUICK DISSOLVE TO:
EXT./INT. TELEVISION STUDIO - SECUIRTY ENTRANCE - MOMENTS LATER
CAMERA (STEADICAM) follows behind Stanley and Rick as they run in from the rain, through some sliding glass doors, past a SECURITY
GAURD who buzzes them into another set of doors --
They enter a hallway with a bunch of production offices, walking swiftly, shaking their wet clothes....the contestant coordinator comes walking towards them: CYNTHIA (30s)

CYNTHIA
There you are, there you are.

RICK
Sorry we're late, Cynthia.

CYNTHIA
Nothin' to it, no problem.
How you doin' Stanley?

STANLEY
I'm fine. Yes. I'm fine.

CYNTHIA
Ready to go,go,go?

STANLEY
Where's Richard and Julia?

CYNTHIA
They're here, they're fine.
In the dressing room.
(to Rick)
See you later --
Rick gives Stanley a pat on the head;

RICK
Go to it, handsome.

STANLEY
See you.
CAMERA holds with Rick, does a 180 around him, he turns his back to us now, walks
a bit, enters a door, into --

THE PARENTS GREEN ROOM
Rick greets the other two kids parents: RICHARD'S MOM (overhweiqht, 50s) and
RICHARD DAD (same) JULIA'S DAD and JULIA'S MOM (50s)

RICK
Who's ready to beat the record?

RICHARD'S MOM
Jesus you scared us!

JULIA'S DAD
That was close.

RICK
It's fuckin cats and dogs out there --

JULIA'S DAD
Cats and Dogs, indeed.
CAMERA picks up with a young PRODUCTION KID who drops some coffee off for
JULIA'S MOM...follow him back out into the hallway -- CAMERA branches off from
him -- moves down another corridor and picks back up with STANLEY and CYNTHIA
as they walk and talk;

STANLEY
Where's the news department at this studio?

CYNTHIA
It's upstairs.

STANLEY
Have you ever been there?

CYNTHIA
Sure, why?

STANLEY
I'm wondering about the weather department. I'm wonderin' wether or not the weather
people use outside meteorlogical services or if they have in-house instruments?

CYNTHIA

I can check on that for you, maybe we can take a tour --

STANLEY
Ok.
They pass CAMERA which picks up now with a woman MARY (40s)
This is Jimmy Gator's assistant...she walks to his dressing room door and knocks --

JIMMY (OC)
Come in.
Mary enters the room. Jimmy is getting dressed in his outfit for the show* and starting
to take shots of Jack Daniel's.

MARY
Rose is on the phone and here's the cards for today --

JIMMY
Fifteen minutes ago, where were those cards?

MARY
I'm sorry.

JIMMY
I need you to get me Paula --

MARY
You want her right now?

JIMMY
Yes. Now. Find her. She's somewhere in the building --

MARY
We're on the air in twenty minutes, Jimmy.

JIMMY
Find her, get her and tell her I want to talk to her, Mary. Fucking hell.
He picks up the phone.

JIMMY
Hello?

INTERCUT:
INT. JIMMY'S HOUSE - THAT MOMENT
CAMERA PUSHES in on ROSE (Jimmy's wife) as she sits in the kitchen on the phone
to him. A MAID does some work in the b.g.

ROSE

How you doing?

JIMMY
I'm drinking.

ROSE
Slowly or quickly?

JIMMY
As fast as I can.

ROSE
Come home soon after the show.

JIMMY
I went to see her -- some fuckin' asshole answers the door in his underwear, he's fifty years old, there's coke and shit laid out on the table --

ROSE
-- did she talk to you?

JIMMY
She went crazy. She went crazy, Rose.

ROSE
Did you tell her?

JIMMY
I don't know. I have to go, I don't have time and I have more drinking to do before I go march --

ROSE
I love you.

JIMMY
Love you too..

ROSE
Bye.
HOLD with Rose.

CUT TO:
EXT. CLAUDIA'S APARTMENT - THAT MOMENT
CAMERA holds a moment on the building. JIM KURRING pulls his squad car INTO FRAME, looks at the building.

CUT TO:
INT. CLAUDIA'S APARTMENT - THAT MOMENT
CAMERA dollies in quick on Claudia as she snorts a line of coke.
She has some music BLASTING.

CUT TO:
EXT. CLAUDIA'S APARTMENT - THAT MOMENT
CAMERA (STEADICAM) follows behind Jim Kurring as he heads up the pathway, up
the stairs and lands at her door. He knocks.

CUT TO:
INT. CLAUDIA'S APARTMENT - THAT MOMENT
Claudia jumps -- turns her head to the door. She sniffs a bit, yells over the blasting
music;

CLAUDIA
...Hello...?

JIM KURRING (OC)
LAPD. Open the door.
She looks through her peep-hole, sees Jim Kurring. She turns looks at her coffee table:
It's full of coke, pills and pot, etc.

CLAUDIA uh...uh...What is it?

JIM KURRING
It's the LAPD, can you open the door, please?
Claudia rushes over to the table of drugs and starts to scoop things up in her arms --

CLAUDIA
Just a minute just a...I have to get dressed -- (fuck,fuck,fuck)

CUT TO:
EXT. MEDICAL BUILDING/SHERMAN OAKS - THAT MOMENT
CAMERA pushes in on LINDA'S MERCEDES as it pulls into a parking structure. The
RAIN is pouring down. She steps out of the car --

CUT TO:
INT. MEDICAL BUILDING - MOMENTS LATER
CAMERA pulls back as Linda exits some elevators, heads down a hall --

CUT TO:
INT. OFFICE/WAITING ROOM - MOMENTS LATER
She enters a psychologist's waiting room. Three or four chairs and a LIGHT SWITCH
that has a doctors name next to it.
ECU - She flips the switch and a red light goes on.

JUMP CUT TO:
INT. PSYCHOLOGIST'S OFFICE - MOMENTS LATER
A small, comfortable office space. Linda is crying, talking, pacing. The psychologist is
a middle aged woman, DR. DIANE.
As they talk, Dr. Diane writes a perscription;

LINDA
I hate doing this, coming here and not being able to talk --

DR. DIANE
I understand, it's fine --
I wish the circumstance was better.

LINDA
I don't know what's gonna happen,
I really don't -- I'm so fucking,
I feel so over the top with everything.

DR. DIANE
Mmm..Hmm. Running out of your medication at all, let alone at a time like this could
be drastic,
I'm glad you came in to see me, as short as this has been --
She hands over the perscriptions (x2) and is about to say another word -- but Linda
SNATCHES the two small pieces of paper from her hand and heads for the door --

LINDA
Thank you Doctor Diane --

SHRINK
Good luck with everything.
ECU - Door slammed.

CUT TO:
INT. EARL'S HOUSE - DEN - THAT MOMENT
CAMERA holds on PHIL. SLOW ZOOM IN as he stands in front of the television,
flipping stations.

ANGLE, THE TELEVISION.
It's plays all sorts of various things. Phil stops a few beats on each thing that looks
vaguely like an infomercial.
He puts the remote down, exits the room. CAMERA stays a moment, catches a glimpse
of a promo for, "What Do Kids Know?"
It's VARIOUS IMAGES of Stanley and the other kids answering questions, with a
calendar showing they've been at it for over seven weeks and total winnings moving
towards $450,000.00

PROMO ANNOUNCER
Can they do it? Tune in live at three o'clock and see if Stanley Spector and his brilliant
friends Richard and Julia can defeat todays adult challengers Mim,
Luis and Todd -- they're moving towards
A Half A Million Dollar Team Total and a "What Do Kids Know?" record --

CUT TO:
INT. EARL'S HOUSE/KITCHEN - MOMENT LATER
Phil enters and picks up the phone. Dials a number. (Director's Note)

INTERCUT:
INT. PINK DOT - THAT MOMENT
A young Mexican GIRL (20's) takes orders for delivery at pink Dot, sits in front of a
little computer.

PINK DOT GIRL
Pink Dot.

PHIL
Hi. I'd like to get an order for delivery.

PINK DOT GIRL
Phone number.

PHIL
818-753-0088.
PINK DOT GIRL
Partridge?

PHIL
Yeah.

PINK DOT GIRL
What would you like?

PHIL
I'd like to get an order of...um...peanut butter.

PINK DOT GIRL
Mmm.Hmmm.

PHIL
Cigarettes. Camel Lights.

PINK DOT GIRL mmm.hmm.

PHIL
Water.

PINK DOT GIRL
Bottled Water?

PHIL
Um, no, y'know what? Forget the water, just give me a loaf of bread...white bread.

PINK DOT GIRL
Ok.

PHIL
And um....do you have Swank magazine?

PINK DOT GIRL
Yeah.

PHIL
Ok. One of those. Do you have Ram Rod?
The magazine, Ram Rod?

PINK DOT GIRL
Yeah.

PHIL
Ok. One of those. And...um...Barely Legal?

PINK DOT GIRL yeah.

PHIL
Do you have that?

PINK DOT GIRL yeah, I said. Is that it?

PHIL
That's it.

PINK DOT GIRL
Do you still want the peanut butter, bread and cigarettes ?

PHIL
Yes. What? Yes.

PINK DOT GIRL

Total is $15.29. Thirty minutes or less.

PHIL
Thank you.
Phil hangs up, looks to Earl. CU - EARL. He's asleep, uncomfortably.
CAMERA moves inside his chest.

QUICK DISSOLVE TO:
INT. EARL'S BODY - THAT MOMENT
CAMERA roams around a bit, watching the CANCER eat away at Earl's lungs.
CAMERA MOVES BACKWARDS, pulling out;

QUICK DISSOLVE TO:
INT. HOLIDAY INN/BANQUET ROOM - THAT MOMENT
CAMERA pulls back from Frank, who heads offstage. The AUDIENCE is applauding
him. The sidekick, DOC takes the mic and makes an announcement about the one hour
break/snacks served in lobby/etc.
Frank hops offstage, greets Captain Muffy and Gwenovier;

CAPTAIN MUFFY
Chief, this is Gwenovier from the show,
"Profiles," for the interview --

FRANK
Hello, hello, I'm a bit out of breath from all this work --

GWENOVIER
That's fine. It's nice to meet you.

FRANK
Are we gonna tape some stuff now?

GWENOVIER
If you're up to it, I've got us set up in a suite upstairs --

FRANK
You got us a room so quick?
Frank and Captain Muffy laugh at the joke.

FRANK
I'm kidding of course.

CUT TO:
INT. HOTEL SUITE - MOMENTS LATER
Frank is getting his mic put on, Gwenovier has a small VIDEO CREW with her. They
both get touched up for the interview, Frank's talking away;

FRANK
I swear to fucking-god, I do one-a-my seminars, I'm Superaman! I'm Batman!
I'm like a fucking action hero the way
I feel afterwards, like I could walk out this door, down the street, pick up any fuckin'
pootie I see that has even one second to stop --
Gwenovier gives a little snap and finger gesture to her CAMERAMAN to start rolling;

GWENOVIER
All it takes is one second?

FRANK
Just one look, one hesitation, one subtle gesture for me to know --
And Bing-Bam-Boom I'm away on a tangent -- I get so fuckin' amped at these seminars
and lemme tell you why: Because I Am What I Believe.
I am what I teach, I do as I say,
I live by these rules as religiously as I preach them: And you wanna know what? I'm
gettin' pussy left, right, up, down, center and sideways.

GWENOVIER
I'm gonna start rolling --

FRANK
-- go, go, go. I'm givin' pearls here.
And I'II tell you samethin' else:
I'm not succeding in the bush because
I'm Frank TJ Mackey. If anything, there are women out there that want to destroy me -
- it makes it twice as hard for me, I run into some little muffin, knows who I am, knows
my schemes and plans -- shit, she's gonna wanna fuck around, prove to her friends, say,
"Yaddda-yadda-yadda, I saw that guy, he wasn't anything, didn't get me." So me?
I'm runnin' on full throttle the whole fuckin' time. Dodging bullets left and right from
terrorist blonde beauties.
But I'II tell you this: The battle of the bush is being fought and won by Team
Mackey. Can I have a cigarette?

GWENOVIER
Ok. So, lemme just ask you a couple questions to start --
Captain Muffy hands Frank a cigarette, lights it for him.
VIDEO CAMERA'S POV - It's zooms in to close up of Frank. He exhales;

FRANK
What do you want to know?

CUT TO:
EXT. SMILING PEANUT BAR - THAT MOMENT

CAMERA BOOMS DOWN and PUSHES IN on Donnie Smith's Honda Accord, with damaged front end, as it pulls into a parking space.
It's POURING RAIN. (dir.note)
CAMERA lands in close. Donnie sits a moment. He plays his tape,
"Dreams," sings along a bit, pep talks himself, does some deep breathing, says;

DONNIE
Make it happen, make it happen and go,go,go.
He gets out of the car real quick --

CUT TO:
INT. SMILING PEANUT BAR - THAT MOMENT
CAMERA (STEADICAM) pushes in as Donnie enters this dark little bar.
It's not too crowded. He takes off his wet coat, brushes his hair back a bit and walks to an empty corner table --
Donnie takes his seat and looks over to the bar -- CAMERA swings a 180, heads away from him -- it moves to the bar area and into:
A young, handsome BARTENDER BRAD (20s) is pouring drinks.
CAMERA picks up with a COCKTAIL WAITRESS (30s) who walks over and brings us back to Donnie's booth --

COCKTAIL WAITRESS
Hello. You're back again, huh?

DONNIE yeah, yes, hi, hello.

COCKTAIL WAITRESS
-- can I get you?

DONNIE
Diet Coke.
She exits. Donnie lights a cigarette -- CAMERA blends from 24fps to 40fps -- he looks across the room -- CAMERA swings 180 back towards the bar and pushes in towards --
Bartender Brad takes the order from the Cocktail Waitress.
He nods, turns from her and smiles to reveal a full set of BRACES.
ANGLE, DONNIE. CAMERA pushes in slow and he smiles, touches his hand to his mouth.
DONNIE'S POV - The Bartender pours the coke, turns his attention towards an old-freaky looking Thurston Howell/Truman Capote/Dorothy Parker type guy (60s) at the end of the bar, who raises his glass, motions as if to say, "Another one of these, please," while waving some money and smiling/flirting with Brad the Bartender.
Donnie's face drops. CAMERA DOLLIES back a little bit and blends from 40fps to 24fps. The Cocktail Waitress arrives back;

COCKTAIL WAITRESS

Diet Coke.

DONNIE
I want a shot of tequila too.

COCKTAIL WAITRESS
-- what kind?

DONNIE
It doesn't matter.
Donnie GLARES across the bar at BRAD and THURSTON as they flirt.

CUT TO:
INT. TELEVISION STUDIO/HALLWAYS - THAT MOMENT
CAMERA leads/follows the kids from the show; STANLEY, RICHARD
(overweight, 12) and JULIA (child-star-type 11). They're led by
CYNTHIA, down the corridors towards the main set --

JULIA
Do you still have to do homework?

RICHARD
Not as much as I used to. Ever since we started, I haven't really gone in to school that
much because I've been getting more and more auditions --

STANLEY
I don't have regular classes anymore.

RICHARD
What do you do?

STANLEY
They just let me have my own study-time, my own reading time in the library.

RICHARD
That's pretty cool.

JULIA
Do you have an agent, Stanley?

STANLEY
No.

JULIA
You should get one, I'm serious, you could get a lot of stuff out of this --

STANLEY
Like what?

RICHARD
What do you mean, "like what?"
-- you could get endorsments and shit --

CYNTHIA
-- Richard.

RICHARD
Bite it, Cynthia. You could get free things from people that want you to endorse their products.

JULIA
Commercials, a sitcom, an MOW or something.

STANLEY
What's MOW?

JULIA
Movie Of The Week. I went up for one this morning with Alan Thicke and Corey Haim
--

RICHARD
Was it a call back?

JULIA
No. But I probably will get a call back.

RICHARD
If we beat the record, you might get a call back --

JULIA
I'll get it because I'm a good actress, Richard.

RICHARD
Saucy-saucy.

CYNTHIA
C'mon guys, settle down --

STANLEY
Cynthia?

CYNTHIA

What?

STANLEY
How much time do we have?

CYNTHIA
Not enough, what do you want?

STANLEY
I should maybe go to the bathroom.

CYNTHIA
Can you hold it?

STANLEY
I don't know.

CYNTHIA
Just hold it, you'll be fine.
They arrive and enter onto the stage -- CAMERA swings around, branches away from them and BOOMS UP to reveal the set;
There is a LIVE STUDIO AUDIENCE that's being settled into their seats.
It's a three-camera set up with a FLOOR DIRECTOR roaming around, shouting orders, etc.
There's a spot for the announcer, an old-pro named DICK JENNINGS (60s)
Dick is in the middle of doing bad-comedy warm up for the studio audience. He's had a few drinks, etc.
The STAGE itself is a cross between JEAPORDY/NEWLEYWED GAME/PRICE IS RIGHT. There's a podium for Jimmy Gator. One panel holds "The Kids," and one panel holds, "The Adults." There are chaser-lights all around and some of the design feels left over from the early days of the show.
CAMERA hangs out with the KIDS as they are ushered into their panel, which at this moment faces away from the audience and is behind a curtain. Julia turns her head, sees something:

JULIA
Here they come --
The ADULT CHALLENGERS are brought out by an assistant type and loaded into their panel. The Adult Challengers are:
Black woman named MIM MacNEAL(40s)
White guy with glasses TODD GERONIMO (20s)
Puerto Rican guy named LUIS GUZMAN (40s)
The Adults give a couple small glares over to the Kids.
RICHARD (sotto)
Yeah, yeah, yeah, keep lookin' tough-old folks.

STANLEY
They look pretty smart, I think.

JULIA
No they don't --

RICHARD
What are they gonna do -- beat us?

STANLEY
Maybe.

JULIA
We're not going out two days before we set the record, it's not gonna happen.

RICHARD
When they want us done, they'll call in the Harvard S.W.A.T team or some shit.
CAMERA lands in CU on Stanley. HOLD. BEAT. THEN:

CUT TO:
INT. JIMMY'S OFFICE - THAT MOMENT
Jimmy and a woman named PAULA (3Os) sit in his office. SLOW DOLLY IN
ON EACH thru scene;

JIMMY
You look great.

BEAT.
PAULA
What the fuck is this, Jimmy?

JIMMY
...you know...

PAULA
Did your wife find out?

JIMMY
No.

PAULA
Then what?

JIMMY
It's just...too late for me to be fuckin' around. I gotta stop.
I gotta clean my brain of all the shit I've done that I shouldn't have done --

PAULA
-- that you shouldn't have done?
That you regret, what? This? What's this? Fuck, man, c'mon. Treat me like an asshole,
but treat me like an asshole.

JIMMY
I don't wanna have to lie to anyone.
I don't want to hurt anyone else, anymore.
She doesn't respond. BEAT. THEN:

JIMMY
Thirty fuckin' years I've been with
Rose, don't -- y'know -- with this, and I know what you think --

PAULA
All your other fluzzies?

JIMMY
Yeah. Yes.

PAULA
You're making me feel so dirty and shitty.
I feel like a big piece of shit right now.

BEAT.
PAULA
Are you gonna tell her what you've done?

JIMMY
Yes.

PAULA
Will you say my name?

JIMMY
If she asks me any question I want to tell her. I want to tell her everything I've done.

PAULA
Well can you do me one favor and don't do that.
Jimmy doesn't answer.

PAULA
Come and tell me it's over and I'll walk away, Jimmy. I've fucked you behind your wife's
back for three years, and you've fucked teenage girls behind mine for the same amount

of time -- I'll walk away, you need something for your life, for your conscience, but don't put me in the middle --

JIMMY
I won't.

PAULA
What happend to you?

JIMMY
I got in trouble at school.
She stands and walks over to him, moves to give him a hug.

PAULA
Are you ok?

JIMMY
Fuck no.
There's a KNOCK at the door and then it's opened by BURT RAMSEY (60s)
He's the producer of the show; (WHIP TO HIM)

BURT
Ready to run. Paula.

PAULA
Burt.
Jimmy takes a quick shot, moves to Paula, gives her a tap on the cheek and says;
JIMMY (to Paula)
You're a good one arentcha?

CUT TO:
INT. TELEVISION STUDIO/HALLWAY - MOMENTS LATER
Burt and Jimmy walking and talking (STEADICAM);

BURT
You smell like trouble --

JIMMY
I'm fuckin' hammered, Burt.

BURT
You ok?

JIMMY ooohhhhhh no.
BURT (re: cards)
Good. You look these over?

JIMMY
It's been the same fuckin' thing for thirty years, Burt --

BURT
These adults are tough enough, I think you'll be surprised -- the Mexican's a bit of a
question mark --
Jimmy FALLS STRAIGHT TO THE FLOOR.

BURT
Fuck - fuck - fuck - Jimmy -

CUT TO:
INT. CLAUDIA'S APARTMENT - THAT MOMENT. **
Claudia finishes throwing her drugs into a dirty t-shirt and throwing that dirty t-shirt
into her laundry basket. Jim Kurring bangs away at the door.

JIM KURRING (OC)
OPEN THE DOOR.
CLAUDIA
I'm coming!
She runs towards the door, takes a small fall on the way, recovers, opens up;

CLAUIDA
Yeah. Hi. Hello.
REVERSE, CLOSE UP - JIM KURRING - 40fps.
CAMERA pushes in on him a little bit at his first sight of Claudia.

JIM KURRING
...yeah...

CLAUDIA
I'm sorry, I had to get dressed.
Wider Angle reveals Jim Kurring, in a bit of a daze, standing with his BILLY CLUB
removed and at the ready. He stands back...they have
SHOUT above the music;

JIM KURRING
-- you the resident here?

CLAUIDA
Yes.

JIM KURRING
You alone in there?

CLAUDIA
Yes.

JIM KURRING
No one else in there with you?

CLAUIDA
No, what's wrong?

JIM KURRING
You mind if I come in, check things?

CLAUDIA
For what?

JIM KURRING
Ok. For one thing, we're gonna need to turn that music down so we can talk, ok?

CLAUDIA
I'm sorry.
She turns and Jim Kurring moves to replace his billy club, but misses the holster and it
FALLS straight to the floor, slides down the steps.
Claudia turns the music down, turns back and sees that he is gone.
Jim Kurring grabs his billy club from the bottom of the steps and bounces back up and
into the apartment as if nothing happend;

JIM KURRING
You live alone?

CLAUIDA
Yes.

JIM KURRING
What's your name?

CLAUIDA
Claudia.

JIM KURRING
Claudia What?

CLAUDIA
Wilson.

JIM KURRING
Ok. Claudia Wilson: You tryin' to go deaf?

CLAUDIA
What?

JIM KURRING
Did you hear what I said?

CLAUDIA
Yeah, but I don't know --

JIM KURRING
-- listenin' to that music so loud:
You Tryin' To Damage Your Ears?

CLAUDIA
No.

JIM KURRING
Well if you keep listenin' to the music that loud you're not only gonna damage your ears
but your neighbors ears.

CLAUDIA
I didn't realize it was that loud.

JIM KURRING
And that could be the sign of a damaged ear drum, you understand?

CLAUDIA
Yeah.

JIM KURRING
You got the TV on too, keep those on at that same time usually?

CALUDIA
I don't know -- I mean. What is this?

JIM KURRING
Have you been drinkin' today, doin' some drugs?

CLAUDIA
No.

JIM KURRING
I got a call of a disturbance, screaming and yelling, loud music. Has there been some
screaming and yelling?

CLAUDIA
Yes. I had someone come to my door, someone I didn't want here and I told them to leave -- so -- it's no big deal.
They left. I'm sorry.

JIM KURRING
Was it a boyfriend of yours?

CLAUDIA
No.

JIM KURRING
You don't have a boyfriend?

CLAUDIA
No.

JIM KURRING
Who was it?

CLAUDIA
I was...he's gone...I mean it's not.
It's over, y'know --
Jim Kurring snoops a bit, she rubs her nose, nervous. Jim Kurring heads closer to bedroom --

JIM KURRING
You mind if I check things back here?

CLAUDIA
It's fine.
Jim Kurring heads into the bedroom, looks around, stands by the laundry basket --

CLAUDIA
What are you lookin' for?

JIM KURRING
Claudia: Why don't you let me handle the questions and you handle the answers, ok?

CLAUDIA ok.

JIM KURRING
You just move in here?

CLAUDIA
About two years ago.

JIM KURRING
Bit messy.

CLAUDIA
Yeah.

JIM KURRING
I'm a bit of a slob myself.

CLAUDIA
Yeah.

JIM KURRING
You and your boyfriend have a party last night?

CLAUDIA
I don't have a boyfriend.
BEAT. Jim Kurring looks at Claudia and she looks back. HOLD.

CUT TO:
INT. SMILING PEANUT BAR - THAT MOMENT.
Donnie sits in his booth after two tequila's. He's slightly fucked up.
He gets up, stumbles over to the bar and takes a seat uncomfortably close to Thurston,
who's now holding court among three or four other
PATRONS. Brad the Bartender is washing glasses, keeps half an eye on things...Donnie
to Thurston;

DONNIE
You look like you've got money in your pocket.

THURSTON
Maybe I'm just happy to see my friend, Brad there.
The PATRONS laugh a bit, Brad nods, Donnie doesn't laugh or look anywhere but
Thurston;

DONNIE
Just throw some money around.
Money, money, money.

THURSTON
This sounds threatening.

DONNIE
Do you have love in your heart?

THURSTON
I have love all over. I even have love for you, friend.

DONNIE
Is it real love?

THURSTON
Well --

DONNIE
-- the kind of love that makes you feel that intagible joy. Pit of your stomach.
Like a bucket of acid and nerves running around and making you hurt and happy and
all over you're head over heels....?

THURSTON
Well you lost me with the last couple of cocktail words spoken, m'boy, but
I believe it's that sort of love.
Sounds nice to me.

DONNIE
I have love.

THURSTON
A very chatty-kind, you do, indeed, it seems.

DONNIE
No. I mean, I'm telling you:
I'm telling you that I have love.

THURSTON
And I'm listening avidly, fellow.

DONNIE
My name is Donnie Smith and I have lot's of love to give.

BEAT.
CUT TO:
EXT. SHERMAN OAKS PHARMACY - THAT MOMENT
CAMERA holds wide angle on a pharmacy. It's still POURING RAIN.
LINDA'S MERCEDES comes driving real fast into FRAME and slams it's brakes on,
parks.

CUT TO:
INT. SHERMAN OAKS PHARMACY - THAT MOMENT.
CAMERA pushes in on Linda as she enters, heads to the back for the perscription
counter and a YOUNG PHARMACY KID behind the counter;

YOUNG PHARMACY KID
Hello.

LINDA
Hi.
She hands over her three perscriptions. The Young Pharmacy Kid takes a long look at them, gives her a suspicious glance.

YOUNG PHARMACY KID
Wow. Lot-o-stuff here, huh?
Linda nods. He goes to the back to the old-guy PHARMACIST and says a few words, points to Linda. Another suspicious look or two from the both of them...the PHARMACIST guy gets on the phone.
ANGLE, LINDA. SLOW ZOOM IN. Blend from 24fps to 40fps.
She just holds her breath and temper, looks down.

CUT TO:
INT. TELEVISION STUDIO/STAGE - THAT MOMENT
CAMERA PUSHES in on a oversized STOPWATCH and the FLOOR DIRECTOR nearby;

FLOOR DIRECTOR
Thirty Seconds.
CAMERA with the announcer DICK JENNINGS who walks to his post.
CAMERA with the ADULT CHALLENGERS who talk a bit amongst themselves,
CAMERA moves over to the KIDS. Richard looks over to Stanley;

RICHARD
The fuck is wrong with you?

STANLEY
I gotta go to the bathroom.

JULIA
Jesus Christ, Stanley.

CUT TO:
INT. PARENT'S GREEN ROOM - THAT MOMENT
CAMERA pushes in on the Parents;

RICK
-- you cannot do that. You have to tone it. Don't be real agressive, just subtely abusive. You must say, "No.
You are not leaving this house until that room is cleaned."

JULIA'S MOM
Julia's room is the same way.

JULIA'S DAD
Like a pig sty. But it's the outfits that we're getting into now --

JULIA'S MOM
You should have seen what she had on walking out the door --

JULIA'S DAD
-- all dolled up.

JULIA'S MOM
I said: "No. No. No. We are not going to a fashion show. You are going to school."

RICHARD'S MOM
-- It's not a fashion show, it's school.

JULIA'S MOM
It is not a fashion show.
CAMERA lands over on Rick, who's flipping through a brocheure for a new MERCEDES.

RICK
Let's make some fuckin' money, folks.
They all look to the Monitor.

WHIP TO:
INT. TELEVISION STUDIO/STAGE - THAT MOMENT
CAMERA pushes in on JIMMY and BURT, behind the curtain. Jimmy drunk;

BURT
You okay? huh? Jimmy?

JIMMY
And the book says: "We may by through with the past, but the past ain't through with us."

BURT
C'mon, Jimmy, snap up, snap up --

JIMMY
In my sleep, Burt.
CAMERA pushes in on the FLOOR DIRECTOR as he counts off;

FLOOR DIRECTOR

And...three...two...one....
He points his finger...CAMERA WHIPS over to DICK JENNINGS who says:

DICK JENNINGS
Live from Burbank, California it's: "What Do Kids Know?"
CAMERA WHIPS RT. to the APPLAUSE signs, then WHIPS again to the AUDIENCE
that cheers, then WHIPS again to see the "What Do Kids Know?" sign as it lowers over
the stage. The THEME MUSIC kicks in and we're away;
Director's Note: We move between their TV CAMERA'S POV and our 35mm

CAMERA POV.
DICK JENNINGS (VO)
Going into our thirty-third year on the air, it's America's longest running quiz show and
the place where three kids get to challenge three adults and in the end see who's boss!
"The Kids" panel as it turns towards the Audience and lights up.

DICK JENNINGS (VO)
Moving towards their eighth consecutive week as champions we have the kids:
Richard, Julia and Stanley.
"The Adults" panel turns towards the audience and lights up.

DICK JENNINGS (VO)
And our new adult challengers today are Todd, Luis, and Mim.

ANGLE - BACKSTAGE - THAT MOMENT
Jimmy stands behind the curtain. CAMERA DOLLIES IN on his back. He holds his
head down.

DICK JENNINGS (VO)
Please say hello and welcome to the always ready host of
"What Do Kids Know?" Your favorite: and my boss: Jimmy Gator!
The curtain opens -- a spotlight SHINES DIRECTLY INTO CAMERA --
Jimmy enters the stage.

CUT TO:
INT. EARL'S HOUSE - LIVING ROOM - THAT MOMENT Sequence D
CAMERA pulls back from the TELEVISION and WHIPS to Phil watching.
The CAMERA pushes past him and over to Earl, asleep in the bed.
Jimmy Gator's opening bit continues OC over the following;

JIMMY GATOR (OC)
Back again, again, again! I'm Jimmy Gator and believe it or not we are at the end of
week seven, going towards eight for these three incredible kids --

WHIP TO:
INT. HOLIDAY INN SUITE - THAT MOMENT

CAMERA pushes in on Frank who's babbling away about "Seduce and Destroy," (Director's Note) then WHIP over to Gwenovier and her video crew as they all listen.

JIMMY GATOR (OC)
-- who hello-hello, are just two days and two games from the "What Do Kids Now?" record for the longest winning streak in this shows thirty three year history --

WHIP TO:
INT. CLAUDIA'S APARTMENT - THAT MOMENT
CAMERA pushes in on Jim Kurring then WHIP to Claudia as they talk and he snoops, etc. (Director's Note: Ref. note pages)

JIMMY GATOR (OC)
We're endorsed by the PTA and the
North American Teacher's Foundation and we are try and do our best to hold standards high -- that's why we're the longest running quiz show in television history --

WHIP TO:
INT. SMILING PEANUT - THAT MOMENT
CAMERA WHIPS from the TELEVISION above the bar which is playing the quiz show and pushes over Donnie, staring at the monitor.
He shots another Tequila.

JIMMY GATOR (OC)
And let me say: With these three kids right here, I wouldn't be surprised if we've got a while to go, but today is a dangerous day --

WHIP TO:
INT. SHERMAN OAKS PHARMACY - THAT MOMENT
CAMERA whips a ZOOMS in slow on Linda, holding her temper as the Pharamcy guy suspiciously glance at her and make a call or two to check on her perscriptions.

JIMMY GATOR (OC)
-- for I have met the three adult challengers backstage and they are quite a challenge for our youngsters -- SO LET'S GET THIS GAME

OFF AND AWAY, EH?
WHIP TO:
INT. JIMMY GATOR'S HOUSE - THAT MOMENT
CAMERA pushes in on ROSE as she watches her husband.

JIMMY GATOR (OC)
Let's jump right in, quick re-cap for those who don't know: Round One.
Three Categories.

WHIP TO:
INT. POLICE STATION - THAT MOMENT
CAMERA pushes in on MARCIE who's being processed and finger printed/ questioned.
Two DETECTIVES nearby/OC throughout. A small portable TELEVISION in the b.g.,
plays the show.

DETECTIVE #1
We want to know where your Son is, Marcie.

DETECTIVE #2
Jerome Samuel Hall. Did he have a fight with your husband? Where they fighting?

DETECTIVE #1
Maybe they had a fight, maybe it was an accident.
Maybe it was an accident?

DETECTIVE #3
Help him out, and help us get there before something else --

DETECTIVE #2
Help us help your son, Marcie.

WHIP TO:
INT. NORTH HOLLYWOOD APARTMENT - THAT MOMENT
CAMERA pushes in on the little kid, DIXON, who gave Jim Kurring the rap earlier.
Sitting around with the friends who we saw earlier in one of their apartments. They're
glued to the
TELEVISION that plays the show.
The BACK OF A FIGURE (black male) enters FRAME and tapes Dixon's shoulder
with a "let's go" motion and Dixon gets up and follows...
CAMERA keeps going in towards the television --

JIMMY GATOR (OC)
Steals are OK, escelating point scale from 25 to 250 so Let's Go Categories!

WHIP TO:
INT. EARL'S HOUSE - LIVING ROOM - THAT MOMENT
CAMERA pushes in profile on PHIL. The DOORBELL RINGS and he jumps.
The DOGS go crazy barking. Phil heads for the door, opens up.
It's the PINK DOT GUY.

PHIL
Hi.

PINK DOT GUY

$15.24.
ANGLE, EARL'S TELEVISION - THAT MOMENT.
A small bank of VIDEO MONITORS pops up and displays some categories;

JIMMY GATOR
We have, "Authors" "The Dee Blue" and "Chaos vs. Superstring"

ANGLE, PHIL
He hands over a twenty dollar bill to the Pink Dot Guy. The DOGS go crazy barking
and he tries to calm them down.

ANGLE, EARL'S TELEVISION
Jimmy behind the podium.

JIMMY GATOR
Adults won a coin toss backstage and they'll have first choice: Todd.

TODD
I'll take "Authors," Jimmy.

ANGLE, PHIL
He dumps the bag out and goes straight for the Porno Magazines.
He flips to the back of one, scanning quickly for something --
XCU, his finger moves down the page, arrives at an AD for "Seduce and
Destroy" that has a picture of Frank with a girl in a bikini and says, "Get Laid Now."

PHIL
Got it.

ANGLE, EARL'S TELEVISION - THAT MOMENT
Jimmy reads from his index cards. (tv slow zoom in)

JIMMY GATOR
First question for 25. This female author's most famous work
"O! Pioneers" --

ANGLE, PHIL - THAT MOMENT
CAMERA pushes in super-quick as Phil picks up the phone and starts to dial the 1-800
number listed in the porno magazine.

CUT TO:
INT. GAME SHOW STAGE - THAT MOMENT
CAMERA does a super fast WHIP and DOLLY in to STANLEY as he presses his
buzzer:

STANLEY

Willa Cather.

CAMERA PUSHES IN ON JIMMY.
JIMMY
For 25. Best known for the "tragedy and blood" genre, this author-playwright --
CAMERA WHIPS and PUSHES IN ON STANLEY.
STANLEY (buzzes)
Thomas Kyd.

JIMMY
This French playwright and actor joined the Bejart troupe of actors --
STANLEY (buzzes)
Moliere.

JIMMY
I'm gonna need a full name, Stanley.

STANLEY
Jean Baptiste Poquelin Moliere.
CAMERA WHIPS to the adults who instantly look un-happy:
LUIS (to Todd)
What the fuck is this?

CUT TO:
INT. PARENTS GREEN ROOM - THAT MOMENT
CAMERA pushes in on Rick as he sits back and smiles.

RICK
My little fucker -- I have no idea where he gets this stuff.

CUT TO:
INT. VAN NUYS OFFICE SPACE - THAT MOMENT
CAMERA pushes in on a geek named CHAD (20s) who answers a phone.
He has a small computer in front of him. This is the bolier-room- answering-phones-
for-orders headquarters for "Seduce and Destroy."
Five or six other guys sit around desks, answering phones and working computers, etc.
There are posters of Frank all around and some maps and some charts, etc.
CHAD (into phone)
"Seduce and Destroy," thisz Chad, can I have your home phone number with area code,
please?

CUT TO:
INT. EARL'S HOUSE - KITCHEN - THAT MOMENT
CAMERA pushes in on Phil, on the phone.

PHIL

Hi, hello, great. This is Seduce and Destroy?

CHAD
It is. Can I have your home phone number with area code?

PHIL
Well I don't want to order anything, you see.
I have a situation, a situation just come up that's really pretty serious and I'm not sure who I should talk to or what I should do but could you maybe put me in touch with the right person if I explain myself?

CHAD
I'm really only equipped to take orders --

PHIL
Well can you connect me to someone else?

CHAD
Well what's the situation?

PHIL
Well, ok. Lemme see how I explain this without it seeming kinda crazy, but here go:
I'm, my name is Phil
Parma and I work for a man named
Earl Partridge -- Mr. Earl Partidge.
I'm his nurse. He's a very sick man.
He's a dying man and he's sick and he's asked me to help him, to help him find his son
-- Hello? Are you there, hello?

CHAD
I'm here, I'm listening.

PHIL
OK. See: Frank TJ Macky is Earl
Partridge's son....

CUT TO:
INT. HOLIDAY INN SUITE - THAT MOMENT
Frank and Gwenovier doing the interview;

GWEN
Where are you from originally?

FRANK
Around here.

GWEN the valley?

FRANK
Hollywood, mainly.

GWEN
And what did your parents do?

FRANK
My father worked in televison.
My mother -- this is gonna sound silly to you -- she was a librarian.

GWEN
Why does that sound silly?

FRANK
Well I guess it doesn't.

GWEN
Does you mother still work?

FRANK
She's retired.

GWEN
Are you close?

FRANK
She's my mother.

GWEN
What does she say about, "Seduce and Destroy."

FRANK
"Go Get 'Em, Honey."

GWEN
And your father?

FRANK
He passed away.

GWEN
I'm sorry.

FRANK people die.

GWEN
I wouldn'tve asked --

FRANK
Not a problem.

GWEN
And you ended up at UC Berkely --

FRANK
From '84 to '89.

GWEN
Psychology major?

FRANK
Right.

GWEN
Do you have your masters?

FRANK
...this close...

GWEN
In five years?
He winks and clicks his teeth.

FRANK
Muffy, can I get another ciggy?

CUT TO:
INT. PHARMACY - THAT MOMENT
The YOUNG PHARMACY KID is stacking some stuff away while waiting for the
PHARMACIST to finish filling the perscription.

YOUNG PHARMACY KID
Cats and Dogs out there, huh?

LINDA mmmhmm.

YOUNG PHARMACY KID
Must have alot goin' on for all that stuff you got back there, eh? You could have quite
a party all that stuff....
Linda looks down. HOLD. BEAT. THEN:

YOUNG PHARMACY KID
You been on Prozac long? Dexadrine?

LINDA
...I don't....

YOUNG PHARAMCY KID
Interesting drugs. Dexadrine's basically speed in a pill. Y'know? But I guess a lot of doctors are balancing out the prozac with the dexadrine, eh?
That Liquid Morphine'll knock you down, out, around, up and down someone's not careful.....can't mix those up, y'know...
...Must have a lot goin' on in your life for all that stuff there.
The Older Pharamacist DINGS his bell and the Young Pharmacy Kid gets the bag and starts to ring it up. SLOW ZOOM IN ON LINDA as he babbles away;

YOUNG PHARAMCY KID (OC)
Strong, strong stuff here, boy...wow....
What exactly you have wrong, you need this stuff?
LINDA snaps. She starts to tremble and cry and build --

LINDA
You motherfucker...you motherfucker....

YOU FUCKING ASSHOLE, WHO THE FUCK ARE YOU?
WHO THE FUCK DO YOU THINK YOU ARE?
YOUNG PHARMACY KID
-- what-what-what, ma'am -- I --

LINDA
I COME IN HERE - YOU DON'T KNOW,
YOU DON'T KNOW WHO THE FUCK I AM
OR WHAT MY LIFE IS AND YOU HAVE THE
FUCKING BALLS, THE INDECENCY TO ASK

ME A QUESTION ABOUT MY LIFE --
Linda PUSHES a large DISPLAY over on it's side, SMASHES things on the counter, throws things around, basically goes nuts. The Older
Pharamacist comes rushing to the front to try and calm things --

OLDER PHARMACIST
Please, lady, why don't you just calm down --

LINDA
And FUCK YOU TOO. Don't you call me "lady."

I come in with these things, I give it over to you, you doubt, you make your phone calls, check on me, look suspicious, ask questions, "I'm sick." I HAVE SICKNESS

ALL AROUND ME AND YOU FUCKING ASK ME MY LIFE?
WHAT'S WRONG? HAVE YOU SEEN DEATH IN YOUR BED
IN YOUR HOUSE? And where is your fucking decency? That I'm asked questions "WHAT'S WRONG?"
You suck my dick, that's what's wrong and you, you fucking call me "lady." You SHAME ON YOU.

SHAME ON YOU. SHAME ON BOTH OF YOU.
She THROWS a crumpled STACK OF MONEY at them both, grabs the PERSCRIPTION and heads for the door --

CUT TO:
INT. LINDA'S MERCEDS - MOMENTS LATER
She slams the door. She's shaking and crying.
CU - Pharmacy bag ripped open.
CU - Bottle cap of Dexadrine popped off.
CU - Linda's mouth as she swallows back the pills.

CUT TO:
EXT. PHARMACY/STREET - THAT MOMENT
CAMERA BOOMS down on her Mercedes as it peel out and off --

CUT TO:
INT. EARL'S HOUSE/VAN NUYS OFFICE SPACE - THAT MOMENT
Continue w/intercut between Phil and Chad on the phone. BEAT, THEN:

CHAD
Why don't they have the same last name?
They don't have the same last name.

PHIL
I know -- and I can't really explain that, but I have a feeling there's something, some situation between them, like they don't really know each other much or well, something like they don't talk much anymore --

CHAD
Uh-huh.

PHIL
Does this sound weird?

CHAD
Well I'm not sure why you're calling me.

PHIL
There's no number for Frank in any of Earl's stuff and he's pretty out of it -- I mean, like
I said, he's dying, y'know. Dying of Cancer.

CHAD
What kind of Cancer?

PHIL
Brain and Lung.

CHAD
My mother had breast cancer.

PHIL
It's rough. I'm sorry, did she make it?

CHAD
Oh, she's fine.

PHIL
Oh that's good.

CHAD
It was scary though.

PHIL
It's a helluva disease.

CHAD
Sure is. So why call me?
CAMERA pushes in on Earl, asleep in the bed, breathing becomes a bit irregular.
HOLD on him. 30fps.

PHIL
I know this all seems silly.
I know that maybe I sound ridiculous, like maybe this is the scene of the movie where
the guy is trying to get ahold of the long-lost son, but this is that scene. Y'know? I think
they have those scenes in movies because they're true, because they really happen.
And you gotta believe me: This is really happening. I mean, I can give you my phone
number and you can call me back if you wanna check with whoever you can check this
with, but don't leave me hanging on this -- please -- please. See: See:
See this is the scene of the movie where you help me out --

CUT TO:
INT. HOLIDAY INN SUITE - THAT MOMENT

Frank and Gwenovier doing the interview, CAMERA DOLLIES IN SLOW ON EACH:

GWENOVIER
-- see, I thought you grew up here in the valley --

FRANK
Like I said, yeah --

GWEN
And you went to Van Nuys High, right?

FRANK
I don't how much I went -- but I was enrolled. I was such a loser back then.
I was -- misguided, pathetic -- I was very fat.
Not even close to what I am today.
Not the Frank TJ Mackey you're eager to talk to because I was swimming in what was
as opposed to I wanted.

GWEN
Where does that name come from?

FRANK
What name? My name?

GWEN
It's not your given name, right?

FRANK
My mother's name, actually.
Good question. You've done you're research.

GWEN
And "Frank?"

FRANK
"Frank" was my mother's father.

GWEN
Ok. That's why. I had trouble locating your school records at Berkely and UCLA.
Your name change -- they had no official enrollment --

FRANK
Oh, yeah. No, no, no. They wouldn't --

GWEN
They wouldn't?

FRANK no, no, no. Certainly not. I wasn't officialy enrolled, that's right.
Was that unclear?

GWEN
Kind of.

FRANK
I wouldn't want that to be misunderstood:
My enrollment was totally unoffical because
I was, sadly, unable to afford tuition up there. But there were three wonderful men who
were kind enough to let me sit in on their classes, and they're names are:
Macready, Horn and Langtree among others.
I was completely independent financially, and like I said: One Sad Sack A Shit.
So what we're looking at here is a true rags to riches story and I think that's what most
people respond to in "Seduce,"
And At The End Of The Day? Hey -- it may not even be about picking up chicks and
sticking your cock in it -- it's about finding What You Can Be
In This World. Defining It. Controling It and saying: I will take what is mine. You just
happen to get a blow job out of it, then hey-what-the-fuck- why-not? he.he.he.

CUT TO:
INT. GAME SHOW SET - THAT MOMENT.
CAMERA pushes in on Jimmy Gator. A BELL is ringing.

JIMMY GATOR
End of Round One! Excellent work ladies and germs, let's see the scores on the boards:
Kids up a leg with 2025, Adults down a bit with 1200. We'll be back for Round Two
and a Ring-Dang-Do --
A sudden and LOUD WISHTLE sounds.

JIMMY GATOR
HELLO! Musical Bonus Question before we go to break and the lucky team is --
Jimmy opens an ENVELOPE and reads:

JIMMY GATOR
Kids in the lead and they get a chance to pull further and farther ahead -- with the
following secret bonus musical question:
I will read you a line from an opera and you are to give me the same line in the language
in which the opera was originaly written and for a bonus
25 you can sing it. Here's the line:
"Love is a rebellious bird that nobody can tame, and it's all in vain to call it, if it chooses
to refuse."
CAMERA PANS and DOLLIES over to the KIDS and moves in close on Stanley;

STANELY

Well that was..uh..in French...and that was in the opera, "Carmen." And that goes...um...
(sings)
L'amour est un oiseau rebelle
Que nul ne peut apprivoiser,
Et c'est bien en vain qu'on l'appelle,
S'il lui convient de refuser.
The AUDIENCE applauds and the "Carmen," que carries over the following scene;

CUT TO:
INT. CLAUDIA'S APARTMENT - THAT MOMENT Sequence E
Jim Kurring and Clauida continued. He walks into the KITCHEN area and sees a pot
of coffee.

JIM KURRING got some coffee brewing, huh?

CLAUDIA
Yeah...it's not...it's been on for a bit --

JIM KURRING
I like iced coffee, generally, but a day like this, rain and what not, I enjoy a warm cup -
-

CLAUDIA
-- do you wanna cup?

JIM KURRING
That's great, thank you.
She starts heating/preparing him some coffee.

CLAUDIA
I don't know how fresh it's gonna be --

JIM KURRING
Oh, it'll be fine, I'm sure, Claudia.

CLAUDIA
You take cream or sugar?

JIM KURRING
That'd be fine. So, Claudia, lemme just say, so I can get my role of LAPD officer out of
the way before we enjoy our coffee (I never like to talk shop over coffee)
I'm not gonna write you up or anything,
I'm not gonna give you a citation here -- but the real problem we have is that there are
people around here, people that work from their homes, people tryin' to get some work
done, and if you're listenin' to your music that loud: They're incovenienced by that. If
you had a job you'd probably understand, but I see you like listenin' to your music and

that's fine, you're just gonna wanna keep it down at a certain volume, maybe memorize
what number you see on the dial and just always put it to that --
If it's the middle of the day -- that's what I do -- just put it on two and a half and that's a
good listening level, alright?
I see you like listenin' to your music loud, but, hey, forget about the neighbors, you end
up damaging your own ears ok?

CLAUDIA
Yeah.

JIM KURRING
Arlight, then. Cheers.
They clink coffee cups. He makes a sour face at the taste;

JIM KURRING
Is this boyfriend bothering you?

CLAUDIA
I don't have a boyfriend.

JIM KURRING
The gentleman who came to the door --

CLAUDIA
-- is not my boyfriend.

JIM KURRING
Many times, in damestic abuse situations the young lady is afraid to speak, but I have
to tell you that, being a police officer, I've seen it happen:
Young woman afraid to speak, next thing you know, I'm gettin' a call on the radio,
I got a 422 --

CLAUDIA
It's not -- what's a 422?

JIM KURRING
It's where situations like these lead, Claudia, unless you do something about it early, if
and when the police call and come for help. Now there are certain measures you can
take --

CLAUDIA
It's not my boyfriend -- and it's not anything -- it's over. Really.
It's not. He won't came back.

JIM KURRING

I don't wanna have to come back here in an hour and find that there's been another disturbance.

CLAUDIA
You won't. You won't have to.

JIM KURRING
But I wouldn't mind comin' back in an hour just to see your pretty face!
They laugh.

CLAUDIA
I'm gonna run to the bathroom real quick.

JIM KURRING
Okey-doke.
She exits. HOLD A BEAT with him.

CUT TO:
INT. CLAUDIA'S BEDROOM - MOMENT LATER
She enters, gets the coke from the laundry basket -- and sets some up, snorts it back --

CUT TO:
INT. CLAUDIA'S KITCHEN NOOK - THAT MOMENT
Jim Kurring looks over his shoulder and sees that she's gone.
He quickly moves to the kitchen and dumps the coffee in the sink and then quickly sits back down. End Carmen Que.

CUT TO:
INT. GAME SHOW SET - THAT MOMENT
CAMERA on Jimmy, behind the curtain, during the Commercial Break.
He takes a shot of Jack Daniels that Mary has brought out for him.

JIMMY
I can't fuckin' do this.

MARY
Are you alright?

JIMMY
Fuck. I think I'm gonna throw up, I think.
(beat)
I haven't thrown up since I was twenty years old.
Jimmy stumbles over to a corner a bit;

ANGLE, GAME SHOW SET.

Stanley is trying to flag down Cynthia, who stands off in the wings, she finally comes over;

CYNTHIA
Stanley, what's the problem?

STANLEY
I have to go to the bathroom, Cynthia.

CYNTHIA
Jesus Christ, Stanley, you can't go to the bathroom now. You have exactly one minute before we're back on the air, this is NOT the time to go to the bathroom.

STANLEY
I'm, I need to go, I'm gonna --

RICHARD
Why does this kinda shit always happen, Stanley?
The Adult Challengers look over at the Kids section;

LUIS
What's the problem over there?

RICHARD
Mind yer bussiness --

MIM
Watch your mouth, little man.

JULIA
Why don't you mind your own bussiness?

CYNTHIA
Alright, stop it, cool down, cool it. Please.
Now: Stanley, you wait until the next commercial break and you can go then -- Just Hold It.
(to Adults)
Don't taunt the kids --

LUIS
I just asked what was going on --

CYNTHIA
Don't start trouble, Luis.

ANGLE, BACKSTAGE.

CAMERA pushes in on Jimmy from behind as he throws up in a corner.
Mary pets his back. He throws up a lot of BLOOD. She snaps fingers to a stage hand to
bring some towles and a glass of water --

OC VOICE
Two minutes, everyone, we're back in two!

CUT TO:
EXT. LAW OFFICE BUILDING/PARKING STRUCTURE - THAT MOMENT
Linda's Mercedes pulls out of the rain and to a parking structure. CAMERA PUSHES
IN real fast, she takes a ticket.
CU'S (Director's note -three ecu's ticket take green button)

CUT TO:
INT. LINDA'S MERCEDES - MOMENTS LATER
CU's on Linda. She pops three or four more DEXADRINE.

CUT TO:
INT. LAW OFFICE BUILDING/HALLWAY - THAT MOMENT
Linda off the elevators...CAMERA pushes in with her....

CUT TO:
INT. LAWYER'S OFFICE - THAT MOMENT
CAMERA whips around, RECEPTIONIST --

LINDA
I'm Linda Partridge to see Alan Kligman.

CUT TO:
INT. SEDUCE AND DESTROY CONDO - THAT MOMENT
CAMERA pushes in quick on a young girl named JANET. (This is the GIRL from
Frank's flashback's.) She answers the phone in this converted condo into office
headquarters for "Seduce and Destroy." Frank TJ Mackey paraphenallia, propoganda
and literature allover the place;

JANET
"Seduce and Destroy," thisz Janet.

INTERCUT:
INT. VAN NUYS OFFICE SPACE - THAT MOMENT
CAMERA pushes in on Chad, on the phone;

CHAD
Hey, Janet, it's Chad.

JANET

What's wrong?

CHAD
Nothing's wrong, I just got some guy on the phone on my other line, he's says he works for this guy, this guy who's Frank's father --

JANET
-- no,no,no what is this? who?
What's this guy's name?

CUT TO:
INT. EARL'S HOUSE - THAT MOMENT
CAMERA (HAND HELD) with Phil, phone to his ear, on hold (we can hear Frank's commercial playing on the receiver, ref. notes.)
Earl is MOANING in pain, the DOGS are barking at the noise.
Earl continues to hallucinate and remains in major pain, but at the same time he's very, very weak. There are moments of strength that pop and push into him and he's very angry with Phil, continues to scream for someone named, "Lily," and generally treats Phil like an enemy.

EARL
LILY. FUCK. LIL, PLEASE. LILY.
Phil moves into the kitchen and gets the bottle of MORPHINE PILLS.
He drops them, the crash on the floor, picks them all up, except one...
...which one of the Mutt Dogs walks over to and eats. Earl SCREAMS.

CUT TO:
INT. SEDUCE AND DESTROY CONDO - THAT MOMENT
CAMERA on Janet on the phone, listens, says:

JANET
...mmm.hmmm. mmm..hmm. Alright.
Put him through and lemme see what's goin' on --

CUT TO:
INT. VAN NUYS OFFICE SPACE - THAT MOMENT
CAMERA on Chad. He puts Janet on hold and clicks over to Phil:

CHAD
Phil, you there?

INTERCUT:
INT. EARL'S HOUSE - THAT MOMENT
CAMERA on Phil, tending to Earl, who moans away. (Bit less pain now.)
The Mutt/Morphine Dog is starting to get a bit wobbly.

PHIL
Yeah, hey. Chad.

CHAD
Alright, so I'm gonna transfer you over to Frank's assitant, Janet she's gonna see what she can do --

PHIL
Thank you, Chad, and good luck to you and your mother --

CHAD
Thank you. Thank you very much.
Chad clicks a line and confrences Janet and Phil.

JANET
Hello?

CHAD
Ok. Janet you have Phil Parma --

JANET
Hello, Phil.

PHIL
Hi, hi, thank you for taking my call --
CAMERA holds with EARL for a quick BEAT, THEN:

CUT TO:
INT. GAME SHOW - BACKSTAGE - THAT MOMENT
Jimmy finishes cleaning himself up and he looks to Mary:

JIMMY GATOR
I have Cancer, Mary.
She doesn't know what to say.

JIMMY GATOR
I have about two months, I have no time.
It's in my bones and I don't have a chance.
And I'm fucked. I had a stroke last week --

MARY
...Jimmy...
The OC call from FLOOR DIRECTOR.

FLOQR DIRECTOR
Ten Seconds.

Jimmy walks from behind the curtain to the "Adult" contestants, takes his mark and waits for the countdown -- CAMERA moves over to Stanley who watches Jimmy closely and sees him stumble a bit, recognizes that something is wrong. Floor Director counts, 3-2-1 --

CUT TO:
INT. SMILING PEANUT BAR - THAT MOMENT Sequence F
CAMERA pulls back from the TELEVISION above the bar, playing the show. We see Jimmy start to chat w/and do intro's for the adults.
(Director's Note: This runs through scene and a complete script is avail/will be shot.)
Donnie and Thurston and the Patrons continued;

DONNIE
....do you know who I am?

THURSTON
You're a friend of the family I presume?

DONNIE
What? What does that mean?

THURSTON
Nothing special, just a spoke in the wheel.

DONNIE
You talk in rhymes and riddles and ra...rub-adub --- but that doesn't mean anything to me, see....see...see I used to be smart....I'm Quiz Kid Donnie Smith.
I'm Quiz Kid Donnie Smith from the tv --

THURSTON
Might of been before my time.

PATRON #1
I remember you. I remember. In the 60's right?

DONNIE
I'm Quiz Kid Donnie Smith.

THURSTON
...like you said...

PATRON #1
Smart Kid! Fuck, yeah, he-he. You got hit by lightning that one time, right?

DONNIE
So what?

PATRON #1
I heard about that.

PATRON #2
Did it hurt?

DONNIE
Yes.

THURSTON
But you're alright now, so what's the what?

DONNIE
What?

THURSTON
That's right.

DONNIE
I used to be smart but now I'm just stupid.

THURSTON
Brad, dear?
Brad turns and looks:

THURSTON
Who was it that said: "A man of genius has seldom been ruined but by himself."

DONNIE
(to himself)
-- Samuel Johnson.

BRAD
I don't know.
Donnie looks up at Brad. Brad smiles with his braces, Donnie looks away quick --

THURSTON
It was the lovely Samuel Johnson who also spoke of a fella "Who was not only dull but a cause of dullness in others."

DONNIE
"The" cause of dullness in others --

THURSTON
Picky, picky.

DONNIE
-- and lemme tell you this: Samuel Johnson never had his life shit on and taken from him and his money stolen -- who took his life and his money? His parents?
His mommy and daddy? Make him live this life like this -- "A man of genius" gets shit on as a child and that scars and it hurts and have you ever been hit by lighting? It hurts and it doesn't happen to everyone, it's an electrical charge that finds it's way across the universe and lands in your body and your head -- and as for "ruined but by himself," not if his parents take his friggin' life and his money and tell you to do this and do that and if you don't? well, what --

PATRON #1
You're parents took your money you won on that game show?

DONNIE
Yes they did.
(turns quick to Thurston)
What does that mean, "spoke in the wheel?"

THURSTON
Things go round 'n round, don't they?

DONNIE
Yes they do, they do, but I'll make my dreams come true, you see? I will.

THURSTON
This sounds Sad as a Weeping Willow.

DONNIE
I used to be smart but now I'm just stupid.

THURSTON
Shall we drink to that?
Donnie looks to the television for a moment, starts to tear up,
CAMERA pushes in slow to an EXTREME CLOSE UP. He repeats line's from his days on "What Do Kids Know?" and does his best Jimmy immitation;

DONNIE
"If a brick weighs one pound plus one half brick -- how much does the brick weigh?"
"Well if subtracting the half of brick from the whole brick you got one half of brick, equals one pound so therefore the brick equals two pounds --" "A little more than kin and less than kind," is Hamlet to Claudius.
"The sins of the father laid upon the children," is Merchant of Venice but borrowed from Exodus
20:5 and "win her with gifts if she respects not words," is Two Gentleman from Verona. Where? Who? How and Why, Kids?

THURSTON
"Why don't you shut the fuck up," is me to you,
Chapter Right Here, Verse Right Now.

CUT TO:
INT. GAME SHOW SET - THAT MOMENT
CAMERA on the set with Jimmy walking over to the "Kids" panel;

JIMMY GATOR
KIDS! Are you guys glued to those seats or what? Are you ever leaving?
You're getting close to the record, do you get more nervous as we go along?

RICHARD
A little --

JULIA
-- yeah....

JIMMY GATOR
-- kids at school must be real excited for you, eh?

JULIA
Oh, yeah...yeah...

RICHARD
Sure.

JIMMY GATOR
Stanley the Man! How are you?

STANLEY
I'm fine. Yes.

JIMMY GATOR
You're fast becoming a celebrity.
How are you handling it all?

STANLEY
Ohh, it's all fine. It's all.
Nice. I'd just like to keep going....keep getting on....

JIMMY GATOR
Sure, sure...that's fine, then...there...with.....
Jimmy starts to loose his grip on the proceedings a bit, slows his pace down....Stanley
notices....

JIMMY GATOR

Well you've got..many..things, many things happening and on the way....

ANGLE, BURT.

CAMERA PUSHES IN on Burt as he sees Jimmy start to zone out a bit.

CUT TO:

INT. JIMMY GATOR'S HOUSE - THAT MOMENT

CAMERA pushes in on Rose, sitting in the kitchen, watching the television. She holds her breath and tears a bit, noticing

Jimmy start to fade.

CUT TO:

INT. GAME SHOW STAGE - THAT MOMENT

Back to Stanley and Jimmy. Jimmy repeats himself;

JIMMY

What were you saying, Stanley?

STANLEY

I was saying...thinking maybe I'd get my own quiz show someday, Jimmy.

Just like you!

The AUDIENCE laughs. Jimmy clicks back with a chuckle and a "isn't that cute," smile to the crowd and he walks over to his podium; CAMERA stays for a moment with Stanley, notices him continue to grab his crotch and make a face....

JIMMY

OK, OK, here we go: Steeper questions, bigger payoff, individual challenges with musical and audio pockets, no-steal-lock-out's, let's get it on in Round Two, Categories are:

CUT TO:

INT. HOLIDAY INN SUITE - THAT MOMENT

Frank and Gwenovier doing the telvision interview. CAMERA DOLLIES

IN SLOW ON EACH:

FRANK

-- that's right, that's right, and what I'M saying, that none of my competitors can say is this: That there is no need for insight or understanding. Things of the past! Gone, Over, Done.

Do you realize how fucking miraculous this is?

How fucking razor sharp and cutting edge and ahead of it's time this concept is? I'm talking about eliminating insight and understanding as human values. GOD DAMN I'M GOOD. There is no need for INSIGHT. There is no need for

UNDERSTANDING. I have found a way to take any subjective human experience --
in other words -- all the terrible shit or all the great shit that you've had happen to you
in your life -- and quickly and easily transform it in the unconscious mind through the
subtle and cunning use of language. The "listener-patient"
(in other words: The Chick) settles into a very light, very delicate, conversationally
induced state: NOT A TRANCE, mind you, but a STATE.
A state that is brand new. The System's state.
What did I do? I REALIZED that concept and put it into practical "get my dick hard
and fuck it" use.
I'm gonna build a state for the seducer and the seducee to live, vote, breath, pay takes
and party
'till dawn. I'm gonna teach methods of language that will help anyone get a piece of ass,
tit and tail --

GWENOVIER
Let's talk about --

FRANK
I just realized this is for television, isn't it? I can't swear up and down like I just did.

GWENOVIER
It's fine. I can bleep it out.

FRANK
I warned you -- I get on a roll...

GWENOVIER
-- let's talk more about your background --

FRANK
Muffy -- coffee?
Muffy moves to pour a cup, Gwen looks down at her clipboard, then:

GWENOVIER
I'm confused about your past is the thing.

FRANK
Is that still lingering?

GWENOVIER
-- just to clarify --

FRANK
So boring, so useless --

GWENOVIER

I would just want to clear some things up:

FRANK
(Muffy delivers coffee)
Thank you, Muffy. Funny thing is:
This is an important element of,
"Seduce and Destory:"
"Facing the past is an important way in not making progress," that's something
I tell my men over and over --

GWENOVIER
This isn't meant --

FRANK
-- and I try and teach the students to ask: What is it in aid of?

GWENOVIER
Are you asking me that?

FRANK
Yes.

GWENOVIER
Well, just trying to figure out who you are, and how you might have become --

FRANK
In aid of what?

GWENOVIER
I'm saying, Frank, in trying to figure out who you are --

FRANK
-- there's a lot more important things
I'd like to put myself into --

GWENOVIER
It's all important --

FRANK
Not really.

GWENOVIER
It's not like I'm trying to attack you --

FRANK

This is how you wanna spend the time, then go, go, go -- you're gonna be surprised at
what a waste it is --
"The most useless thing in the world is that which is behind me," Chapter Three --

GWENOVIER
We talked earlier about your mother.
And we talked about your father and his death.
And I don't want to be challenging or defeatist here, but I have to ask and
I would want to clarify something -- something that I understand --

FRANK
I'm not sure I hear a question in there?

GWENOVIER
Do you remember a Miss Simms?

FRANK
I know alotta women and I'm sure she remembers me.

GWENOVIER
She does. From when you were a boy.

FRANK
Mm. Hm.

GWENOVIER
She lived in Tarzana.

FRANK
An old stomping ground --is this the "attack" portion of the interview,
I figured this was coming sooner or later -- Is "the girl" coming in for the kill?

GWENOVIER
No, this is about getting something right and claryfying one of your answers to an earlier
question --

FRANK
Go ahead and waste your time.

GWENOVIER
I was told that your mother died.
That your mother died when you were young --

FRANK
And that's what you've heard?

GWENOVIER

I talked to Miss Simms. Miss Simms was your caretaker and neighbor after your mother died in 1980.
BEAT. Frank goes silent.

GWENOVIER

In my research I have you listed as the only son of Earl and Lily Partridge.
(beat)
And what I learned from Mrs. Simms is that your mother passed away in 1980.
(beat)
See: It's my understanding that the information supplied by you and your company and answers to question's I've asked are incorrect, Frank.
And if I'd like to get to the bottom of who you are and why you are then I think your family history -- you're accurate family history...well: this seems important...Frank...?

VIDEO CAMERA POV - THAT MOMENT
Frank lights his cigarette. CAMERA zooms into CU.

FRANK

Are you asking me a question?

GWEN

Well I guess the question is this:
Do you remember Miss Simms?

BEAT. HOLD, THEN:
CUT TO:
INT. GAME SHOW SET - THAT MOMENT
Jimmy asks questions. Stanley is visibly uncomfortable;

JIMMY

Kids, Adults, I'd like you to put yourself at a picnic. Place yourself there with your family and friends if you'd like -- you'll hear three musical notes and you are to tell me what it might represent that you'd find at a picnic -- The First Three Notes:
OC we hear three musical notes. The "Adults" panel lights up,
Todd answers;

TODD

Well, Jimmy, I know this, I have perfect pitch, you see -- and that would be A-D-E.
And that would represent lemonade.

JIMMY

For 250. Next notes, please:
OC musical notes: E-G-G.
TODD (buzzes)
Got it. That's E-G-G which would be ~egg."

Richard and Julia glance at Stanley, like "why the fuck aren't you answering these questions?" He looks straight ahead.

JIMMY
For 500 and the Third Set Of Notes:
OC musical notes: B-E-E.
TODD (buzzes)
B-E-E -- and don't get stung.
The "Adults" are now within 200 points of the "Kids," on the scoreboard.

CUT TO:
INT. LAWYERS OFFICE - THAT MOMENT
Linda seated across from a lawyer, ALAN KLIGMAN (50s) She's visibly shaking and fucked up.

KLIGMAN
You don't want any water?

LINDA
No...I just...(starts crying a bit)
I'm so fucked up here Alan, I don't know...there's so much...so many things --

KLIGMAN
Are you on drugs right now?

LINDA
If I talk to you...y'know...if I tell you things...then you're a lawyer, right?
You can't say things, you can't tell anyone, it's like the privelage, right?
Attorney-client, you understand?

KLIGMAN
Not exactly, Linda. I'm not sure where you're going with this --

LINDA
Like a shrink, like if I go to see a shrink, I'm protected, I can say things -- fuck -- I don't know what I'm doing --

KLIGMAN
Linda, you're safe. Ok. It's alright.
You're my friend. You and Earl are my clients and what you need to talk about won't leave this room, you have something you have to say --

LINDA
-- I have something to tell you.
I have to tell you something.
I want to change his will, can I change his will?...I need to ---

KLIGMAN
You can't change his will. Only
Earl can change his will.

LINDA
No, no....no, you see...I never loved him.
I never loved him, Earl. When I started, when I met him, I met him and I fucked him
and I married him because I wanted his money, do you understand?
(beat)
I'm telling you this now...this I've never told anyone...I didn't love him.
And now....I know I'm in that will,
I know, I was there with him, we were all there together when we made that fucking
thing and all the money I'II get -- I don't want it -- Because I love him so much now...I've
fallen in love with him now, for real, as he's dying, and I look at him and he's about to
go, Alan, he's dead...he's moments...
(beat)
I took care of him through this, Alan.
And What Now Then?

CUT TO:
INT. GAME SHOW STAGE - THAT MOMENT
CAMERA pushes in on Jimmy.

JIMMY
Let's listen:
There's an OC VOICE that speaks the clue;

VOICE
"Hello, Mary. How are you and the seven kids? As you probably heard by know, we
sure gave that Pope a run for his money --"
The ~Adults" buzz. Jimmy looks to Mim.

MIM
Well: That would be General Robert
E. Lee. His wife Mary Park Custiss.
And he did have seven children and he would be talking about Pope, who he defeated
at the Battle of Monasses --

CUT TO:
INT. PARENTS GREEN ROOM - THAT MOMENT
CAMERA pushes in on Rick, who sits back, starting to get real pissed that Stanley isn't
answering these questions.

RICK
C'mon, c'mon, c'mon, snap out of it.

CUT TO:
INT. GAME SHOW STAGE - THAT MOMENT
CAMERA moves from the AUDIENCE over to the Stage, listening to another question
that is spoken by the OC voice -- this time in French;
VOICE (in French)
"Hello, Josephine,
I'm speaking from Egypt --"
The Adults buzz again and Mim answers;

JIMMY
Mim --

MIM
Well that would be Napoleon speaking to Josephine.

JIMMY
That's right!
ANGLE, BURT. He stands off, looking at the scoreboard as the
Adults have now pulled ahead by 200 points...he mumbles and grumbles to himself.

CUT TO:
INT. LAWYER'S OFFICE - THAT MOMENT
Linda continued with the lawyer, Kligman.

LINDA
I don't want him to die, I didn't love him when we met, and I've done so many bad things
to him that he doesn't know, things I want to confess to him, but now I do: I love him.
I love him so much and I can't stand -- he's going.

KLIGMAN
What kind of medication are you on right now, Linda that's --

LINDA
This is not any fucking medication talking, this isn't -- I don't know.
I don't know -- Can you give me nothing?
You have power of attorney, can you see him, can you, in this final fucking moment,
go see him and make sure --- change the fucking will -- I don't want any money, I
couldn't live with myself, this thing I've done --
I've fucking done so many bad things --
I fucked around. I fucked around on him,
I fucking cheated on him, Alan. You're his lawyer, our laywer, THERE, I'm his wife,
we are married.
I broke the conract of marriage, I fucking cheated on him, many times over, I sucked
other men's cocks and fuck - fuck - fuck -
....fuck....

Other Things I've Done..

KLIGMAN
Adultery isn't illegal -- it's not something that can be used in a court to discredit the will
or -- Linda. Linda. Calm down.

LINDA
I can't.

KLIGMAN
You don't have to change the will, if what you want to do is get nothing you can
renounce the will when it's time.

LINDA
Where will the money go?

KLIGMAN
Well. Considering that there's no one else mentioned in the will...we'd have to go to the
laws of intestacy, which is -- as if someone died without a will --

LINDA
What does that mean?

KLIGMAN
The money would go to Frank. The court would put the money in the hands of a relative
--

LINDA
-- that can't happen. Earl doesn't want him to have the money, the things.

KLIGMAN
-- unless Frank is specifically ommitted as a beneficiary that's what will happen.

LINDA
This is so over-the-top and fucked-up
I can hardly stand it.

KLIGMAN
Linda, you just have to take a moment and breath and one thing at a time --

LINDA
Shut the fuck up.

KLIGMAN
I'm trying to help, Linda --

LINDA
Shut the fuck up. Shut the fuck up.

KLIGMAN
You need to sober up.

LINDA
Now you must really shut the fuck up, please.
Shut The Fuck Up.

KLIGMAN
Linda --

LINDA
I have to go.
She heads for the door.

KLIGMAN
Let me call you a car, Linda.

LINDA
Shut the fuck up.
She's out the door.

CUT TO:
INT. GAME SHOW STAGE - THAT MOMENT
Three MEN in TUXEDOS and HARMONICAS have taken a place near the band.
Jimmy, reading from his cards, introduces them and asks the following question:
(Note: Jimmy's speech is starting to slur a bit more at this point. His motor skills seem
to be fading quickly.)

JIMMY
Imagine you are attending a jam session of classical composers and they have each done
an arrangment of the classic favorite, "Whispering." Here are three variations on the
theme, as three classic composer's might have written it -- you are to name the
composer. The First:
The Harmonica Fella's play an arrangment....CAMERA pushes in close on STANLEY
and TITLS DOWN CLOSE TO HIS PANTS....
Stanley begins to piss his pants. He trembles and shakes and holds back tears as the wet
stain gets bigger.
OC through this we hear the Adults answer the question:

TODD (OC)
Well, Jimmy that sounded to me like Brahms, a bit like his Hungarian
Dance Number Six, I believe.

JIMMY (OC)
Excellent. Next number:
The Harmonica Fella's play another arrangment of "Whispering" that sounds like Ravel's "Bolero."
Stanley moves his arms down to his sides to cover his crotch and pull at his pants -- and his BUZZER goes off with a brush of the side of his arm --

JIMMY
Stanley the Man -- answer:
Stanley. HOLD. He starts to cry. Julia and Richard look over at him and see his pants and they start to laugh a bit.

STANLEY
...I don't know the answer...
Jimmy starts to STUDDER and SHAKE a bit....holds a tight grip on the podium;

JIMMY GATOR
That is not right! That's not right,
Stanley, the answer is...Ravel....Ravel....
....xhjksndlsmnop.....
CAMERA WHIPS and pushes over to the FLOOR DIRECTOR.

FLOOR DIRECTOR
What the fuck is wrong with him?
(into headseat}
What do you wanna do here, he's fading fast --

CUT TO:
INT. BOOTH - THAT MOMENT
The main booth with monitors and board, etc. The DIRECTOR and and ASSITANT watch the monitors;

DIRECTOR
I need a better cutaway, go to the black chick, Camera Three, Camera Three the black chick --
A monitor sees the video camera zoom in on Mim as a cutaway but her face is like, "What the fuck is going on?"

CUT TO:
INT. GAME SHOW SET - THE FLOOR - THAT MOMENT
Jimmy is, with a lot of trouble, trying the Harmonica
Fella's with the next question...
...Burt walks over quickly to the Floor Director...

BURT
Get the technical difficulty card up --

...CAMERA pushes over to Stanley, who's crying and shaking....
...CAMERA pushes in on Jimmy, who stumbles back from his podium and falls to the ground....taking the podium with him....
...CAMERA pushes in on Burt and the Floor Director...

BURT
Cut it, go to the card, go to the fucking card --

CUT TO:
INT. BOOTH - THAT MOMENT
The DIRECTOR snaps his fingers to an ASSISTANT at the board.

DIRECTOR
Go to the card, now -- go --

CU - MONITOR IMAGE.
The card that reads, "Technical Difficulty," comes up and holds.

CUT TO:
INT. CLAUDIA'S APARTMENT - THAT MOMENT
CAMERA pushes in real quick on Claudia SNORTING COKE from her hand in the bedroom -- she rushes back into the kitchen area --

CLAUDIA
Ok, ok. I'm back.

JIM KURRING
This is, for not a fresh cup, a great cup of coffee, Claudia --

CLAUDIA
Thank you.
She sits down, ready to talk, lights a cigarette.

CLAUDIA
What do you wanna talk about?

CUT TO:
INT. GAME SHOW STAGE - THAT MOMENT
Burt, Mary and Assistants and folks run over to Jimmy. He stands, doesn't realize what's happend and mumbles, "what the fuck, what the..."
The AUDIENCE is murmuring, standing and watching the scene.

CUT TO:
INT. HALLWAY - THAT MOMENT
CAMERA leads RICK as he comes charging out of the green room and races down the hallway --

CUT TO:
INT. GAME SHOW SET - THAT MOMENT
CAMERA with the "Kids" panel as Richard and Julia looking at Stanley.

RICHARD
Did you piss your fuckin' pants, Stanley?

STANLEY
Shut up -- shut up --
Cynthia walks over;

CYNTHIA
What happend, what's going on?

STANLEY
NOTHING. NOTHING HAPPEND. GO AWAY.
CYNTHIA
Don't tell me to go away, Stanley.
I am the Co-ordinator in this show and you will answer the questions that I ask, you
understand?
Rick comes over;

RICK
What's the problem, what's the problem here?

STANLEY
I'm fine. nothing.

RICK
Why didn't you answer those questions?

STANLEY
I didn't know the answer --

RICK
Bullshit. Bullshit. You know the answer to every goddamn question and
I knew the answer to those questions and I'm not half as smart as you are so
What Happened?

STANLEY
I don't know.

RICHARD
He pissed his pants.

RICK
Did you -- did you --

STANLEY
I didn't I'm fine, I'm fine.

RICK
Stand up.

STANLEY
I said I'm fine.
Rick grabs Stanley a bit and sees a large WET STAIN in Stanley's pants.

RICK
...oh Jesus, what the fuck...?

STANLEY
I'm fine. I'm fine, I just wanna keep playing --

RICK
Why did you do this?

ANGLE, JIMMY. THAT MOMENT.
Jimmy is sweating.

JIMMY
I had a stroke, I think I had a stroke.

BURT
Call 911. Call 911 right now.

JIMMY
No, no, no. I'm fine. It's small,
I wanna keep going --

BURT no, no, c'mon Jimmy we need to call this quits and you need to see a doctor.

JIMMY
I'm telling you right now, I'm fine.
I lost my goddamn balance and I couldn't see a moment, but I'm ok.

BURT
Call 911, Mary, do it right now.

JIMMY

You fuckin' don't do that. You don't do it, you cocksucker. I'll fuckin' kill you with my barehands. Go. get the fuck fuck -- we're going back and we finish the show --

BURT
Jimmy you look like you're about to fuckin' die right here --

JIMMY
Shut it. Shut yer fuckin' mouth.
ANGLE, RICK and STANLEY.

RICK
Are we gonna keep going with this game?

STANLEY
Yes.

RICK
You're two fuckin' days from the record, get through this and I'II do anything for you, you just gotta get through this --

STANLEY
Alright.

RICK hang in there, ok. I love you.
Rick walks away with Cynthia...
...Dick Jennings has sobered up a bit and is doing bad, "calm down/comedy/everything's cool" stuff for the Audience....
...Jimmy and Burt and Mary stand up and a MAKE UP person runs over with some water and cleans him up a bit. Burt moves away --

FLOOR DIRECTOR
What are we doing?

BURT
This is fuckin' stupidity, we'll get back on and go through it --
The Floor Director starts throwing directions in his headset and to the camera people, etc.

CUT TO:
INT. HOLIDAY INN SUITE - THAT MOMENT. Sequence G
CAMERA holds on Frank and starts a SLOW DOLLY IN. Gwenovier remains OC.

GWENOVIER (OC)
Frank...Frank...what are we gonna do here?
Are we having a staring contest?
(beat)

Do you have anything to say?

CAPTAIN MUFFY (OC)
I think maybe we should rap this up, Chief --
Frank SNAPS his fingers and signals captain Muffy to stay quiet.

GWENOVIER (OC)
I'm not trying to attack you, Frank.
I think that if you have something that needs to be cleared up...Well, then...
(beat)
I was told that your father, (your father is Earl Partridge,) that he left you and your
mother and you were forced to take care of her during her illness...that you took care of
your mother as she struggled with Cancer....
(beat)
And Miss Simms became your caretaker after your mother died...Frank...Frank...
(beat)
Frank, can you talk about your Mother?
(beat)
Frank....can you?

CAMERA LANDS CU. ON FRANK. HOLD, THEN:
CUT TO:
INT. CLAUDIA'S APARTMENT - THAT MOMENT
Claudia and Jim Kurring talking. She's rubbing her jaw, blabbing away and he's
listening with a grin;

CLAUDIA
--- yeah, yeah, I get in it in my ear.
It's TMJ is what it's called technically.

JIM KURRING
What's that stand for?

CLAUDIA
Tempural-something-mandibular, thing with something, I dunno.
But it affects my ear, I don't even know if I have TMJ exactly but just very tight, like -
it's like a muscle spasm and it's just gets so clenched --
She's interupted by the call on his RADIO. He takes the call.
(Director's Note: Technical blah-blah-blah,etc.)

JIM KURRING
This is my job.

CLAUDIA
We were just gettin' warmed up.
We were just getting started.

JIM KURRING
Well if you listen' to that music too loud again and that fella returns maybe we'll share
another cup of coffee --

CLAUDIA
If you're not here for a 422 --

JIM KURRING
No. No. Don't joke about that.
That's not funny, Claudia. Please, now.

CLAUDIA
I'm sorry.

JIM KURRING
Ok, then. Keep your chin up and your music down, alright?

CLAUDIA
Yes. I will. It was nice to meet you
Officer Jim.

JIM KURRING
Just Jim.

CLAUDIA yeah, good, ok.

JIM KURRING
Bye, bye, Claudia.

CLAUDIA
Good bye.
She closes the door. HOLD.

CUT TO:
EXT. CLAUDIA'S APARTMENT - THAT MOMENT
Jim Kurring stands outside the door for a moment. He hesitates a moment, then....he's
about to knock....His RADIO goes off...he turns it down real quick --

CUT TO:
INT. CLAUDIA'S APARTMENT - THAT MOMENT
Claudia hears the RADIO go off and stands back a bit from her door...hold a
moment...then there's a KNOCK...she opens up:

CAMERA DOLLIES IN A LITTLE ON JIM KURRING.
JIM KURRING

I'm sorry, Claudia.

CLAUDIA
What is it? Did you forget something?

JIM KURRING
No, no. I was wondering...man oh man.
I think I feel like a bit of a scum-bucket doing this, considering that I came here as an officer of the law and the situation and all this but I think I'd be a fool if I didn't do something I really want to do which is to ask you on a date.

CLAUDIA
You wanna go on a date with me?

JIM KURRING
Please, yes.

CLAUDIA
Well...is that illegal?

JIM KURRING
No.

CLAUDIA
Then...I'd like to go...What do you want to do?

JIM KURRING
I don't know. I haven't thought about it -- you know what -- that's not true -- I have thought about it. I've thought about going on a date with you since you opened the door.

CLAUDIA
Really?

JIM KURRING
Yeah.

CLAUDIA
I thought you were flirting with me a little.
He laughs and she laughs and then:

CLAUDIA
Do you wanna go tonight? I mean, are you working?

JIM KURRING
No, I'm off tonight. I would lov-like, to go tonight, I can pick you up,
I can pick you up here at about what time? What time?

CLAUDIA
Eight o'clock?

JIM KURRING
What about ten o'clock, is that too late? I don't get off and then --

CLAUDIA
Oh sure yes, that's fine, late dinners are good. Should I get dressed up or -- ?

JIM KURRING
No, no, just casual maybe, maybe
I thought -- there's a spot I like to go, it's real nice that overlooks a golf course and the
course is lit up at night --

CLAUDIA
Billingsley's?

JIM KURRING
Yeah, You know it? You know Billingsley's?

CLAUDIA
It's my favorite place --

JIM KURRING
Oh, see? This is great. Ten o'clock.

CLAUDIA
Great, bye.

JIM KURRING
Bye.
She closes the door.

CUT TO:
INT. HOLIDAY INN/SEMINAR ROOM - THAT MOMENT
CAMERA pushes in on DOC, who's speaking to a group of Frank's disciples. He's blah-
blah-blahing about Seduce and Destory, etc.

DOC
Not true. Not true. And you know what?
Even if you don't get to pump her, you can still practice honing your skills on a femenist
--

DISCIPLE
-- I know --

DOC
-- and you need to do that.

DISCIPLE
I will.

DOC
No, you need to do it.
His CEL PHONE rings and he excuses himself.
DOC (into phone)
Thisz Doc.

INTERCUT:
INT. SEDUCE AND DESTROY CONDO - THAT MOMENT
CAMERA on JANET. She's on the phone. It rings.

JANET
Doc it's Janet.

DOC
What's up?

JANET
I have to talk to Frank, is he nearby?

DOC
He's doing the interview with the lady --

JANET
I need you to interupt him, I need to get him on the phone with me right away --

DOC
What happend?

JANET
Doc, go get Frank and put him on the phone.

CUT TO:
INT. HOLIDAY INN SUITE - THAT MOMENT
CAMERA pushes in on Gwenovier and Frank. (Dead on Singles.)

GWENOVIER
C'mon, Frank. What are you doing?

FRANK

What am I doing?

GWENOVIER
Yeah.

FRANK
I'm quietly judging you.

CUT TO:
INT. GAME SHOW STAGE - THAT MOMENT
CAMERA pushes in on the FLOOR DIRECTOR again who counts down;

FLOOR DIRECTOR
And...three...two...one ---
He points to Jimmy, who pops into shape, looks into the TV CAMERA.

JIMMY GATOR
What a day and what a round, going back and in for me and the final speed round to determine who's who today -- scores on the board's Kids:
9225. Adults: 11,000. And this game is not out of reach for the Kids...can they hang in there and break the record? (etc,etc)
Elders! Who's the lucky so and so?
Mim from the "Adults" speaks into her mic.

MIM
It's gonna be me, Jimmy.

JIMMY
C'mon down here, Mim.
She stands up and crosses over to Jimmy. This is for a ONE ON ONE final section speed round. One Kid vs. One Adult.

ANGLE, STANLEY.
CAMERA pushes in on him and lands in CU.
He takes his shirt out of his pants and tries to pull it down enough to cover the large wet stain in his pants.

ANGLE, JIMMY AND MIM
They chat about the game so far, etc. "They're quite a challenge, etc."
ANGLE, STANLEY and RICHARD and JULIA.
Stanley can't pull his shirt down enough to cover. He turns to
Richard and Julia;

STANLEY
I don't wanna go, I can't do it this time.

RICHARD
-- the fuck are you talking about?

JULIA
You have to go, Stanley. You're the smartest.

STANLEY
I don't wanna do it. Why can't one of you do it --

RICHARD
Stanley if you don't fuckin' stand up and go over there I'm gonna beat your ass --

STANLEY
I'm sick of being the one, the one who always has to do everything, I don't want to be the one always --

JIMMY (OC)
KIDS!
Jimmy looks over to the "Kids" panel.

JIMMY
Do I even have to ask? Stanley, get your butt over here --
Stanley looks like a deer in headlights. The AUDIENCE applauds.

CUT TO:
INT. SMILING PEANUT BAR - THAT MOMENT
The TELEVISION above the bar holds this moment where Stanley won't move. DONNIE is seriously fucked up now and the CAMERA pushes in on him. He glances around, up the television, sees Stanley. BEAT.
Thurston and the other folks around chat away, etc;

DONNIE
...I'm sick....I'm sick here now.....
They continue to chat, trying to ignore him now;

DONNIE
I confuse melancholy and depression sometimes....

THURSTON
Mmm.Hmm.

DONNIE
You see?

THURSTON
Why don't you run along now friend, your dessert is getting cold.

DONNIE
I'm sick.

THURSTON
Stay that way.

DONNIE
I'm sick and I'm in love.

THURSTON
You seem the sort of person who confuses the two.

DONNIE
That's right. That's the first time you're right. I CONFUSE THE TWO

AND I DON'T CARE.
Donnie looks to Brad, then:

DONNIE
HEY. HEY.
Brad looks. Donnie stands up, backs away from the bar as he talks;

DONNIE
I love you. I love you and I'm sick.
(beat)
I'll talk to you....I'll talk to you tommorrow. I'm getting corrective oral surgery
tomorrow. For my teeth. For my teeth and for you....for you so we can speak.
You have braces. Me too. Me too. I'm getting braces, too. For you. For you, dear Brad.
And I don't have any money. And I don't have any money now but I'll get it...I will for
you, Brad. I love you, Brad. Brad the Bartender.
(beat, crying now)
You wanna love me back? Love me back and I'll be good to you. I'll be god damn good
for you.
And I won't be mad if you don't know who said what.
I won't punish you if you get the answer wrong.
I can teach and tell you: Samuel Johnson.

THURSTON
Brad, honey, you have a special secret crush over here I think, don't take him too lovely
-- he might get hurt --

DONNIE
You mind your own bussines.

THURSTON

Gently, son --

DONNIE
Brad, I know you don't love me now --

THURSTON
"It's a dangerous thing to confuse chidlren with angels..."

DONNIE
-- and you wanna know the common element for the entire group, like he asks...I'll tell you the answer: I'll tell you, 'cause I had that question. I had that same question....Carbon.
In pencil led, it's in the form of graphite and in coal, it's all mixed up with other impurities and in the diamond it's in hard form.
(Jimmy impersonation)
"Well...all we were asking was the common element, Donnie...but thank you for all that unnecessary knowledge...ahhh, Kids! Full of useless thoughts, eh?" Thank you. Thank you.
(beat)
And the book says: "We may be through with the past but the past is not through with us."
(to Thurston)
And NO IT'S NOT DANGEROUS TO DO THAT.
Donnie has backed away, close to the bathroom. He heaves a bit, cries, turns and runs for the bathroom --

CUT TO:
INT. SMILING PEANUT/BATHROOM - THAT MOMENT

OVERHEAD ANGLE, LOOKING STRAIGHT DOWN ONTO:
Donnie bursts in the bathroom and starts to vomit and moan, etc.

CUT TO:
INT. POLICE CAR - MOVING - THAT MOMENT
It's pouring RAIN still. Jim Kurring is talking to himself, doing
"Cops." (Dial: Ref. improv. notes/sweet girl/excited/date/job)
Jim Kurring interupts himself and notices something (very blurry, through the RAIN)
JIM'S POV: A young BLACK MALE (late 20s) is standing on the street, about to jay-walk.
The Young Black Male, at the site of Kurring, turns around and walks back the direction he came, deciding against the jay walk.
Jim Kurring looks in his rear view mirror and sees that the Young
Black Male is now RUNNING back towards something --

CUT TO:
EXT. STREET - THAT MOMENT

Jim Kurring's POLICE CAR makes a U-turn.

CUT TO:
INT. CLAUDIA'S APARTMENT - THAT MOMENT
Claudia snorts a line of coke, comes up and looks at her televison;
It's playing, "What Do Kids Know?"

CUT TO:
INT. GAME SHOW SET - THAT MOMENT
Stanley doesn't move. He says to Jimmy:

STANLEY
I'm going to pass, Jimmy.
ANGLE, JIMMY. He doesn't know what to do and he's a bit out of it.

JIMMY
Stanley, passing to one of the other kids --

RICHARD
We want Stanley to go, Jimmy.

STANLEY
I don't want to go.

BEAT.
CUT TO:
INT. HOLIDAY INN/LOBBY - THAT MOMENT
CAMERA (STEADICAM) follows/leads DOC as he walks from the seminar area to
the elevators...this is one continuous shot...as he gets into the elevator's and rides up,
talking on the cel phone.

DOC
I'm walking towards the elevator's, Janet.

JANET (OC)
Fine. Phil, you still there?

PHIL (OC)
Yeah I'm here.

JANET (OC)
I wanna ask you one question, Phil:
Have you talked to anyone else about this? About Frank and Earl?

PHIL (OC)
No I haven't.

JANET (OC)
Alright, good, I'd like to keep it that way -- all the security and what not, you understand? This could be a delicate situation for Frank and the family --

DOC (OC)
What happend?

JANET (OC)
Doc, just - don't, how close are you?

DOC (OC)
I'm about to get off the elevator --
The Elevator doors DING and OPEN and Doc steps out -- heads down the hallway towards the suite --

JANET (OC)
Phil, hang in just one more minute ok? I'm gonna put you on hold -- Doc you still there?

DOC
Yeah, I'm here, I'm off the elevator, walking down the hall, now --

CUT TO:
INT. GAME SHOW SET - THAT MOMENT
Stanley doesn't move. Jimmy tries to hold it all together;

JIMMY
Richard, Julia, kids? What's it gonna be, we need a player for one on one --

RICHARD
We want Stanley to play, Jimmy and we're not sure why he won't --

STANLEY
I don't want to play. I always play, I always answer the questions and I don't wanna do it anymore --
CAMERA pushes in on Burt, who snaps at Cynthia:

BURT
What the fuck is he doing, what's wrong with him?

CYNTHIA
I have no idea.

CUT TO:
INT. HOLIDAY INN - HALLWAY - THAT MOMENT

CAMERA (STEADICAM) following Doc as he walks swiftly down the hallway towards the suite --

CUT TO:
INT. EARL'S HOUSE - THAT MOMENT
CAMERA on Phil on the phone. He sits watching Earl. 30fps. PUSH IN.

CUT TO:
INT. EARL'S HOUSE - GARAGE - THAT MOMENT
It's black. The GARAGE DOOR opens....Linda's MERCEDES is pulling in out of the POURING RAIN....

CUT TO:
INT. BOOTH - THAT MOMENT
The DIRECTOR and his ASSISTANT and other folks in the booth;

DIRECTOR
This fuckin' kid ain't gettin' up and we don't have a show, live television, ladies and gents --

CUT TO:
INT. PARENTS GREEN ROOM - THAT MOMENT
The other parents snap at Rick. CAMERA DOLLIES in on him slow.

JULIA'S MOM
What the hell does he think he's doing?

RICHARD'S DAD
Is this a point? is this a game?

RICK
GET THE FUCK UP, KID.
CUT TO:
INT. HOLIDAY INN SUITE - THAT MOMENT
CAMERA on Frank. He looks at his watch, then:

FRANK
Time's up. Thank you for the interview.

GWENOVIER
So you sat it out, that's what you did?

FRANK
You requested my time and I gave it you, you called me a liar and made accusations. And you say, "If I'd known I wouldn't have asked," then it's not an attack? Well, I don't wanna be the sort of fella who doesn't keep his word. I gave you my time, Bitch.

So fuck you now.
Frank heads out of the room quick. CAMERA leading him in CU.

GWENOVIER
You're hurting a lot of people, Frank --

FRANK
-- fuck you.
He's out the door with Captain Muffy in tow.

CUT TO:
INT. HALLWAY - THAT MOMENT
CAMERA moving quick with Doc towards the room. Frank and Captain Muffy step
out of the room and Doc holds up the Cel Phone....stops.

DOC
Frank, there's a situation on the phone --

CUT TO:
INT. EARL'S HOUSE - THAT MOMENT
The DOGS go crazy barking and Phil jumps a bit. They hear the garage door and run
towards it. The Morphine Dog runs into a wall.
Phil turns his head (40fps)

CUT TO:
INT. GAME SHOW SET - THAT MOMENT
CAMERA on Stanley. BEAT. HOLD.

JIMMY (OC)
I need a player, Kids....c'mon now.
(to Audience)
The indescision of a child, ladies and germs!
The AUDIENCE laughs a bit and chuckles.

STANLEY
This isn't funny. This isn't "cute."
Jimmy -- Jimmy -- we're not a toy -- we're not dolls, here. This isn't funny you see, the
way we're looked at if you think that we're cute Because What?
What? I'm made to feel like a freak if I answer questions and I'm smart or
I have to go to the bathroom. What Is That?
(starts to cry)
And what is that, Jimmy, I'm asking?
I'm asking what is that, Jimmy?
I'm asking you that -- ?
CAMERA pushes in a bit on him.

JIMMY
Well I'm not sure, Stanley.

CUT TO:
EXT. APARTMENT BUILDING/LA RIVER - THAT MOMENT
CAMERA {STEADICAM) follows Jim Kurring as he walks around the side of an apartment building, looking for the BLACK MALE....he snoops a bit, holding his flashlight as it's just about dark....the side of the building runs along the L.A River.....he starts in towards something...
A very LOUD GUNSHOT IS HEARD and HITS on the side wall of the apartment, right next to Jim Kurring's FACE --
...he ducks for cover, looses balance and falls down, in the mud, sliding down the embankment next to the L.A. River --- another
GUN SHOT is heard....
Kurring reaches for his REVOLVER which is not in it's holster --

CUT TO:
INT. SMILING PEANUT/BATHROOM - THAT MOMENT
CAMERA zooms in from overhead angle as Donnie continues to throw up violently.

CUT TO:
INT. HOLIDAY INN - STAIRWELL - THAT MOMENT (INTERCUT)
CAMERA holds on Frank in close up, he's on the phone.
Doc and Captain Muffy stand with him in the stairwell.

JANET (OC)
I'm sorry, Frank. I didn't know what you would want here, what you would want me to do -- I'm -- I asked him all the right questions, he's his nurse, he's sitting right there with him and he's -- I mean,
I can hear him in the background -- your father --

FRANK
Is he at the house?

JANET (OC)
I asked him the exact adress and he gave it -- I know that this must be hard, you having to hear this --

FRANK
Don't give me things, Janet just tell me the thing, the information --

JANET (OC)
I'm sorry.

CUT TO:
INT. EARL'S GARAGE - THAT MOMENT

Linda parks the car and leaves the ENGINE RUNNING. BEAT.
We can hear the DOGS BARKING OC....HOLD.

CUT TO:
INT. GAME SHOW SET - THAT MOMENT
Stanley is continuing. He's hyperventilating.

STANLEY
We are not on display. I am not a doll.

**I AM NOT A DOLL....I' M NOT SILLY AND CUTE.
I'M SMART SO THAT SHOULDN'T MAKE ME SOMETHING,
SOMETHING SO PEOPLE CAN WATCH HOW SILLY IT
IS THAT HE'S SMART? I KNOW. I KNOW THINGS.
I KNOW. I HAVE TO GO TO THE BATHROOM I HAVE
TO GO TO THE BATHROOM AND I HAVE TO GO.
JIMMY**
I'm sorry, Stanley.
Stanley embarresed now.

STANLEY
I'm sorry, I'm sorry, I didn't mean to do this.

CUT TO:
INT. PARENTS GREEN ROOM - THAT MOMENT
RICK is standing now....he VIOLENTLY throws a chair against the wall and it
SHATTERS into a hundred pieces --

**RICK
FUCK. FUCK. FUCK. FUCK.
CUT TO:**
EXT. APARTMENT/LA RIVER EMBANKMENT - THAT MOMENT
It's FLOODING with RAIN....Jim Kurring is without gun and he's scared shitless....and
he can't see...and he's running for cover in some bushes....CAMERA is HAND HELD
and wild, following and falling with him....MUD and RAIN and SHIT everywhere......
His POV...across a bridge...he sees the slight FIGURE as it flees....
(could be the Black Male, but hard to tell in a quick glimpse) he then sees another
SMALLER FIGURE scuttle away...
He doesn't run.....he stays...holds....

CUT TO:
INT. CLAUDIA'S APARTMENT - THAT MOMENT
CAMERA pushes in on her cocaine on the table, TILTS up to her FACE, watching the
show, then WHIPS RT. and pushes in towards the MONITOR.

ON THE MONITOR.

Stanley is crying....

CUT TO:
INT. GAME SHOW SET - THAT MOMENT
CAMERA on Stanley.

STANLEY
I don't mean to cry, I'm sorry.

JIMMY
It's okay, Stanley. It's alright.
CAMERA with Burt as he walks to the Floor Director...

BURT
Take us off the air, go to the the credits --
The Floor Director starts to speak some things into the headset.

CUT TO:
INT. EARL'S GARAGE - THAT MOMENT
Linda rolls down the windows in the closed garage with the engine running...fumes start
to fill the garage...she starts to cry and lights a cigarrette...the bag of perscriptions sits
next to her...

CUT TO:
INT. STAIRWELL - THAT MOMENT (INTERCUT)
Frank on the phone with Janet, Captain Muffy and Doc in stairwell.

FRANK
I haven't spoken to this asshole in ten years....what did I do....?
What did I do today for this? For all of this? ....what....is this....
....Is This A Movie.....?

CUT TO:
INT. GAME SHOW SET - THAT MOMENT
The MONITORS in the place go to a Still Card that has the
"What Do Kids Know?" logo...and the titles start to roll on it.
Stanley notices and he RUNS from the podium, towards backstage...
...Jimmy is standing next to Mim he holds on to her a moment..... loosing his balance
again....
....Burt and Cynthia rush the stage....
Stanley dissapears from the stage...

CUT TO:
INT. EARL'S HOUSE - THAT MOMENT
Phil still on the phone, Earl is asleep. He stands up and heads for the garage -- hears the
sound of the engine running -- dogs are continuing to bark like crazy --

CUT TO:
INT. GARAGE - THAT MOMENT
Linda in CU. She hesitates a moment. THEN: She quickly shuts off the engine, GRABS
the bag of LIQUID MORPHINE --

CUT TO:
INT. EARL'S HOUSE - THAT MOMENT
CAMERA leads/follows Linda as she enters, approaches Phil;

PHIL
Linda --

LINDA
What are you doing?

PHIL
I've got Frank...Frank Earl's son.
He's...he asked me to get him and I did --

LINDA
Hang up the phone.

PHIL
No, Linda, you don't understan --

LINDA
PUT THE FUCKIN' PHONE DOWN, HANG IT UP.
She SLAPS his FACE HARD. The PHONE FALLS to the ground.

CUT TO:
INT. STAIRWELL - HOLIDAY INN - THAT MOMENT (INTERCUT)
Frank on the cel phone to Janet --

FRANK
Put him on --
Janet clicks Frank over and there's a MOMENT of BLUR/NOISE (Linda and
Phil, screaming and static) and then it's gone --

CUT TO:
INT. EARL'S HOUSE - THAT MOMENT
Linda screaming at Phil.

LINDA

You don't do that, you don't call him, you don't know to get involved in the bussiness of his, of his of my family. this is the family, me and him do you understand? You understand? NO ONE ELSE.
THERE IS NO ONE ELSE. That man, his son does not exist. HE IS DEAD. HE IS DEAD and WHO TOLD YOU TO DO THAT?

PHIL
Earl asked me, Linda, please, Linda,
I'm sorry -- Earl asked me --

LINDA
**BULLSHIT. BULLSHIT HE DIDN'T ASK YOU,
HE DOESN'T WANT HIM, HE DOESN'T
WANT TO TALK TO HIM, SO FUCK YOU THAT
HE ASKED THAT. THERE IS NO ONE BUT ME
AND HIM.**
She breaks down, more, more, more.

CUT TO:
INT. STAIRWELL - THAT MOMENT (INTERCUT)
Frank listens on the phone to dead air....hold a long moment, then:
He hands the phone back to Doc;

FRANK
There's no one there.
Frank walks away quick. CAMERA leads him out of the stairwell and down the hallway...HOLD ON HIS FACE CLOSE.

CUT TO:
INT. GAME SHOW STAGE - THAT MOMENT
CAMERA (STEADICAM) follows Mary as she runs over to Jimmy.

JIMMY
Take me outta here, Mary...I gotta go, I gotta go home to Rose, please, please.
She leads him away. CAMERA moves over to BURT who's dealing with the situation -- RICK comes running over, looking for Stanley.
"Where is he? Where the fuck did he go?" Burt tries to calm him down.
CANERA moves over to Cynthia who's dealing with Richard and Julia and Mim and Luis and Todd.

CYNTHIA
Let's go, c'mon, get up --

RICHARD
Did we win or lose, I mean --?

CYNTHIA
I don't know, Richard, they need to talk it over --

LUIS
You lost, kid. They go to the score at the time it was called --

JULIA
That's not an official rule.

LUIS
That's the way it goes.

RICHARD
Bullshit. Who says that, what rule book, in what sport? This is different, it's a quiz show, they don't go by sports rules --

MIM
Let's all just settle down --

CYNTHIA
Richard, shut it and keep it down.

RICHARD
If he hadn't pissed his pants, we woulda won. We fucking had this game.

LUIS
You didn't have shit, kid.
CAMERA with Jimmy and Mary as they head off, down the HALLWAY and towards some elevators -- He's really out of it --

CUT TO:
INT. CLAUDIA'S APARTMENT - THAT MOMENT
She sits in front of the coke and in front of the television.

CU. TELEVISION IMAGE - THAT MOMENT
A still card with the "What Do Kids Know?" logo and the credits still running. At the end a logo that reads:
This has been a Big Earl Partridge Production

CUT TO:
EXT. WASH AREA/APARTMENT - DAY
CAMERA (HAND HELD) with Jim Kurring. He's searches around frantic for his revolver....looking everywhere...RAIN IS POURING.
He does tearful "cops" dial. Ref: "I'm not goin' back to the Station House without my god damn gun." etc.

CUT TO:
EXT. STREETS/BURBANK - THAT MOMENT
CAMERA tracks with Stanley as he runs and runs down the streets in the RAIN.
CAMERA holds a ECU as we move.

CUT TO:
EXT. SMILING PEANUT/PARKING AREA - THAT MOMENT
Donnie walks out and gets in his car -- he goes to start it, but it won't start. HOLD
outtside the car. Rain pouring down.
He gets out and walks. A Pedestrian walking in to the bar recognizes him and smiles,
says:

PEDESTRIAN
Smart Kid Donnie Smith! Quiz Kid! He.He.
Donnie keeps walking straight past.

CUT TO:
INT. EARL'S HOUSE - THAT MOMENT
Linda is bedside with Earl. She cries her eyes out. She speaks to him in mumbles about
"...sorry..." "...my love..."
"...you've lived a long, good life..." She prepares the bottle of liquid morphine and sets
it next to the him...HOLD.
Earl comes out of it a bit, pets her head, mumbles a few words that don't make sense.
Phil in the b.g. Linda can't administer the drops, she turns quickly to Phil;

LINDA listen...listen to me now, Phil:
I'm sorry, sorry I slapped your face.
...because I don't know what I'm doing...
...I don't know how to do this, y'know?
You understand? y'know? I...I'm...I do things and I fuck up and I fucked up....forgive
me, ok?
Can you just...

PHIL
....it's alright....

LINDA
Tell him I'm sorry, ok, yes, you do that, now, I'm sorry, tell him, for all the things
I've done...I fucked up and I'm sorry....
And I'm Gonna Turn Away And Walk Now And Not
Look At Him Not See My Man, My Earl, I'll leave now...and tell him it's ok and I'm ok.
The whole thing was ok with me -- and I know.
She turns quick and walks out of the house.
HOLD ON PHIL. He paces around a moment or two, looks at the side table.

CU - THE BOTTLE OF LIQUID MORPHINE.

It's ready to go.
CU - PHIL. He looks at it.

CUT TO:
INT. HOLIDAY INN - SEMINAR ROOM - THAT MOMENT
CAMERA holds on the image of a slide that reads:
"How To Fake Like You Are Nice And Caring"
Frank steps into FRAME. HOLD. OC we hear the audience applaud.

FRANK
Welcome back. Back from break.
I hope you guys stayed away from those little nacho bits I saw out there...
I know...I know...hey, you're not payin' for the snacks....
Slight laughter. Frank slows down.

FRANK
"How To Fake Like You Are Nice and Caring."
This is...obviously...quite an important section...I mean, let's face it...face the facts...Men Are Shit, right? I mean, that is what they all say. We've all done bad things...bad things that no woman has ever done...that's what they say.
We As Men are taught to apologize: "I've done wrong."
"I'm sorry." "My needs as a man made me..."
Something, something...bullshit....well what
I would like to say....
Frank references some note cards, a bit of a daze is clear now:

FRANK
If you feel, made to feel like you need them, like -- like you can't live if you're without them or you need, what?
They're pussy? They're love? Fuck that.
Self Sufficient, gents. That's the truth.
What you are -- we are -- you need them for what? To fucking make you a piece of snot rag? A puppett? huh? Hear them bitch and moan? bitch and moan -- and we're taught one thing -- go the other way -- there is No Excuse I will give you,
I'm not gonna apologize -- I'm not gonna apologize for my NEED my DESIRE...my, the things that I need as a man to feel comfortable...
You understand? You understand? You need to say something, "my mommy hit me or daddy hit me or didn't let me play soccer, so now I make mistakes, cause a that -- something, so now I piss and shit on it and do this."
Bullshit. I'm sorry. ok. yeah. no. fuck. go. fuck. alright. go make a new mistake. maybe not, I dunno...fuck....
Frank drops the microphone and walks off stage...Audience rumbles with confusion, etc. Doc and Captain Muffy frantic, etc. Frank heads off -- slight look across the reception hall to see Gwenovier --
He's gone.

CUT TO:
INT. EARL'S HOUSE - THAT MOMENT Sequence H
CAMERA on Earl. He opens his eyes a bit....looks over to Phil.

EARL
Phil...Phil...
Phil comes over and takes a seat next to him.

EARL
I'm onna try and talk...I'm atryan say some thing some thing...
Earl begins to talk. (Director's Note: Following is the story Earl tells, it is to be more broken and elliptical, factoring in Earl's state of mind and health, etc, but here's the concept in its entirety;)

EARL
Do you know Lily? Phil..do you know her?

PHIL
No.

EARL
...Lily...?

PHIL
No.

EARL
She's my love...my life...love of it...
In school when you're 12 years old.
In school, in six grade....and I saw her and I didn't go to that school...but we met.
And my friend knew her...I would say,
"What's that girl?" "How's that Lily?"
"Oh, she's a bad girl...she sleeps with guys..." My friend would say this....but then sometime...I went to another school, you see?
But then...when high school at the end, what's that? What is that? When you get to the end?

PHIL
Graduation?

EARL
No, no, the grade...the grade that you're in?

PHIL
Twelve.

EARL

Yeah...So I go to her school for that for grade twelve...and we meet...she was fuckin...like a doll...porcelain doll...and the hips...child bearing hips...y'know that? So beautiful.

But I didn't have sex with anyone, you know? I was not...I couldn't do anything...always scared, y'know... she was...she had some boyfriends...they liked her y'know...but I didn't like that.

I couldn't get over that I wasn't a man, but she was a woman. Y'see? Y'see I didn't make her feel ok about that....I would say, "How many men you been with?"

She told me, I couldn't take it...take that

I wasn't a man....because if I hadn't had sex with women...like as many women as she had men...then I was weak...a boy....

But I loved her...you understand?

....well, of course, I wanted to have sex with her...and I did and we were together....we met...age twelve, but then again...age seventeen...something, somethin...

I didn't let her forget that I thought she was a bad...a slut.....a slut I would call her and hit her....I hit her for what she did...but we married...Lily and me and we married...but I cheated on her...over and over and over again...because I wanted to be a man and I couldn't let her be a woman...a smart, free person who was something...my mind then, so fuckin' stupid, so fuckin....jesus christ, what would I think...did I think....?

...for what I've done...She's my wife for thirty eight years...I went behind her... over and over...fucking asshole I am that I would go out and fuck and come home and get in her bed and say

"I love you..." This'z Jack's mother.

His mother Lily...these two that I had and I lost .... and this is the regret that you make...the regret you make is the something that you take...blah...blah...blah... something, something.....

(beat)

Gimme a cigarettee?

Through the following Phil tries to give Earl a cigarette, which Earl can't get to his mouth, but then mimes that he's smoking as he starts to get more and more delusional, etc.

EARL

She had cancer...from her...in her stomach and I didn't go anywhere with her...and I didn't do a god thing... for her and to help her....shit...this bitch...the beautiful, beautiful bitch with perfect skin and child bearing hips and so soft...her namewasLilysee?

(beat, fading)

He liked her though he did, his mom,

Frank/Jack...he took care of her and she died.

She didn't stick with him and he thinks and he hates me, ok...see...I'm...that's then what you get?

....are you still walkin' in that car...?

PHIL

What? Say it again...walking in the car?

EARL

....getthat on the tv....there...

Earl starts to break down in tears, streaming out of his eyes, his body isn't moving at all;

EARL

...mistakes like this are not ok... sometimes you make some, and ok...not sometimes to make other one....know that you should do better....I loved Lily.

I cheated on her. For thirty five years.

And I have this son. And she has cancer.

And I'm not there. And he's forced to take care of her. He's fourteen years old to take care of his mother and watch her die on him.

Little Kid. And I'm not there. And She Dies.

And I Live My Life. And I'm Not Fair.

Thirty eight years and she has cancer and

I'm gone...I leave...I walk out, I can't deal with that...who am I? Who the fuck do I think I am to go and do a thing?

Shit on that and that lovely person.

I'll go away...I'll go away...I can't hold this..you gotta take this fuckin' pen outta my hand...you fuckin' piss, cocksucker...

.....atke this.....

Phil mimes as if he's taking a pen from Earl's hand.

PHIL

I got it.

CAMERA stays with PHIL. Hold on him as Earl continues a moment.

SLOW DOLLY IN.

EARL

OH FUCK...THIS FUCKIN STORY HAS FALLEN APART and I don't even think I can...I got no punchline -- we had good times later, the best times, the love of my life, I thirty eight years -- but never the respect and the...she knew what I did...she knew... all the stupid things I've done but the

LOVE was stronger than anything you can think up.

CAMERA LANDS CU ON PHIL. Earl's voice continues over the following:

CUT TO:

EXT. JIMMY GATOR'S HOUSE - THAT MOMENT/EVENING

Jimmy and Mary pull up in the pouring rain. Rose comes out and they help him in the house.

EARL'S VOICE

...The attachment....I loved her so much.

And I didn't treat her and the goddamn regret...THE GODDAMN REGRET...and I'll die...

CUT TO:
INT. JIMMY GATOR'S HOUSE - THAT MOMENT/EVENING
Rose and Mary help Jimmy to the couch and get him situated.

EARL'S VOICE
Now I'll die and I'll tell you: what?
The biggest regret of my life:
I let my love go.....

CUT TO:
INT. CLAUDIA'S APARTMENT - THAT MOMENT/EVENING
Claudia in the shower. Claudia brushinq her hair in the mirror.
Claudia attempting to look nice. Claudia, dressed for the date, sits in front of the coke
and looks at it;

EARL'S VOICE
...I ruined my love...jesus...jesus christ. what did I do and I had to get away...?
something, something to do....I can't explain.
....I love her so much....leave her there.... and to punish...punish her....

CUT TO:
INT. POLICE CAR - THAT MOMENT/EVENING
Jim Kurring on the radio of his squad car, reports the gun missing.
(Technical language here.)

EARL'S VOICE
....and the punishment for what? What?
...nothing....and I'm so embarresed.... so embarresed for what I've done...

CUT TO:
INT. WASH AREA/APARTMENT BUILDING - THAT MOMENT/EVENING
Other OFFICERS assist in the search for the missing gun. They are out with flashlights,
etc. A severe search of the area is underway. Jim
Kurring is clearly getting a lot of shit from the other officers, etc.

EARL'S VOICE
I'm seventy five years old and embarresed.
....million years ago...my fuckin REGRET
AND GUILT AND these things...don't let anyone tell you that you shouldn't regret
anything.....don't do that...don't.....

CUT TO:
INT. POLICE STATION/REPORT WRITING ROOM - LATER/EVENING
CAMERA pushes in on Jim Kurring, in civilian clothes now, filling out a Loss Report.
CU's on the form. OC voices of officers making fun of him, etc. CAMERA continues a

bit past him, views, through some window, MARCIE...across the way in a detaining room.

EARL'S VOICE
...you fuckin' regret what you want...
...use that....use that....

CUT TO:
INT. HOLDING ROOM - THAT MOMENT
CAMERA pushes in on Marcie. She's crying and looking down.
She lifts her head, speaks to an UNSEEN OFFICER nearby, guarding her cell;

MARCIE
I wanna confess what I've done.

CUT TO:
INT. SCHOOL LIBRARY - THAT MOMENT/EVENING
Stanley breaks a window. Stanley reaches in and unlocks a lock.
Stanley rummages around the dark school library. He's soaking wet...he accumulates a bunch of books and starts to search for stuff....CU - Dissolve images, optical, etc. (child performers,etc)

EARL'S VOICE
....use that regret for you any way you want...you can use that ok.... someone says not to regret or think about the past, something, mistakes we make.....bullshit.

CUT TO:
INT. DONNIE SMITH'S APARTMENT - THAT MOMENT/EVENING
Donnie takes some KEYS out of a kitchen drawer and puts them on his key chain. Donnie places the keys on one by one....

EARL'S VOICE
....this is a long way to go for no punch...a little moral....story I say...
Love. love. love....this fuckin' life.... ohhhhhhh, love.....

CUT TO:
EXT. EMPTY PARKING LOT - THAT MOMENT/EVENING/NIGHT
CAMERA holds a wide angle. Linda's Mercedes is parked.

CUT TO:
INT. LINDA'S CAR - THAT MOMENT/EVENING/NIGHT
Linda takes some pills. Then she takes some more...then she takes some more....then she swallows a whole bottle of pills...she drinks from a small bottle of Vodka....swallows every last pill.....

EARL'S VOICE

...it's so fuckin' hard....and so long.... life ain't short it's long....Life is long, godddmnit -
- god damn....whatd I do?
Whatd I do? ohhhh what'dIdo?

CUT TO:
INT. FRANK'S CAR - THAT MOMENT/NIGHT
CAMERA holds CU on Frank. He just sits. BEAT. THEN.

WIDER ANGLE, THAT MOMENT.
Reveal that Frank's car is sitting out front of Earl's house.
The Mexican Nurse that we saw earlier in the film, who Phil relieved, walks past his
car and up to Earl's house...

CUT TO:
INT. EARL'S HOUSE - MOMENTS LATER/NIGHT
Phil quietly stands in the front doorway, sotto words with the
Mexican Nurse, who keeps outside.

PHIL
It's ok...I'm gonna stay...stay it out.
The Mexican Nurse nods, understands. Phil turns back into the house.

CUT TO:
INT. EARL'S HOUSE - THAT MOMENT/NIGHT
CAMERA CU on the bottle of liquid morphine. Phil's hand comes into FRAME and
takes it....TILT up to his face.
Phil is in tears....he dips the baby dropper in the bottle.....
Earl is out of breath, painfully....Phil hesitates, then:
CU - The liquid morhphine is dropped into Earl's mouth.

CUT TO:
INT. CLAUDIA'S APARTMENT - THAT MOMENT/NIGHT
She looks at the coke in front of her. She hesitates. Her stereo is playing a song....it
plays softly, then gets a bit louder....
She leans down and SNORTS the fat line of COKE. HOLD on her....she starts to sing
along with the song....

CLAUDIA
"..it's not what you thought when you first began it...you got what you want.... now you
can hardly stand it though by now you know, it's not going to stop....."
The SONG continues. The following has each of the principles half singing along with
the song, who's lead vocal will stay constant throughout.

CUT TO:
INT. JIM KURRING'S APARTMENT - THAT MOMENT

CAMERA PUSHES in slowly on Jim Kurring. He sits on the bed, dressed up and ready to go. He starts to sing along to the song as well.

JIM KURRING
...it's not going to stop...it's not going to stop 'till you wise up..."

CUT TO:
INT. JIMMY'S HOUSE - OFFICE - THAT MOMENT
CAMERA moves in towards Jimmy, alone, sitting in his office, singing.

JIMMY GATOR
"You're sure there's a cure and you have finally found it"

CUT TO:
INT. DONNIE'S APARTMENT - THAT MOMENT
CAMERA pushes in on Donnie smith as he starts to sing.

DONNIE SMITH
"You think....one drink...will shrink
'till you're underground and living down, but it's not going to stop..."

CUT TO:
INT. EARL'S HOUSE - THAT MOMENT
CAMERA DOLLIES in on Phil, holding back his tears and singing along to the song...as he sits over Earl....

PHIL
"It's not going to stop...it's not going to stop...."
CAMERA moves over to Earl, eyes closed, starts to sing as well...

EARL
"...it's not going to stop 'till you wise up..."

CUT TO:
INT. EMPTY PARKING LOT - THAT MOMENT
CAMERA DOLLIES in on LINDA. She's passed out in her car, head pressed against the glass, but she starts to sing along....

LINDA
"...prepare a list of what you need before you sign away the deed, 'cause it's not going to stop..."

CUT TO:
INT. FRANK'S CAR - PARKED - THAT MOMENT
CAMERA pushes in a bit on Frank, singing along.

FRANK
"...it's not going to stop...it's not going to stop....it's not gonna stop 'till you wise up, no it's not gonna stop..."

CUT TO:
INT. SCHOOL LIBRARY - THAT MOMENT
CAMERA pushes in, (light coming up from the book he reads) optical, glimpse what he reads....then pulls back from STANLEY.

STANLEY
"..till you wise up, no it's not going to stop, so just....give up."

PULL BACK.
CUT TO:
EXT. SKY - NIGHT Sequence I
The rain stops. Suddenly and quickly it's over. Clear as a bell. HOLD.
Title card: Weather information,etc.

CUT TO:
INT. CLAUDIA'S APARTMENT - STAIRWELL - NIGHT
The door opens and Claudia looks really nice. Jim Kurring smiles and says hello.

CUT TO:
EXT. CLAUDIA'S APARTMENT - MOMENTS LATER
Jim Kurring opens the door for Claudia and she gets in.
He runs around and they drive off.

CUT TO:
INT. DONNIE'S APARTMENT - THAT MOMENT
Donnie takes the KEYS and puts on big dark coat and looks in the mirror.

DONNIE
You know, you know, you know. Go,go,go.

CUT TO:
INT. DONNIE'S APARTMENT - STAIRWELL - THAT MOMENT
Donnie knocks on his neighbor's door. A little OLD LADY opens up;

LITTLE OLD LADY
Donnie, oh, Donnie --

DONNIE
Hello, dear...I need a favor.

CUT TO:
EXT. DONNIE'S APARTMENT - CAR PORT - THAT MOMENT

Donnie comes down and gets in the little old lady's
Buick Regal and starts it up.

CUT TO:
EXT. EARL'S HOUSE - THAT MOMENT
Frank gets out of his car and walks up to the house.
He rings the doorbell.

CUT TO:
INT. EARL'S HOUSE - THAT MOMENT
The DOGS go crazy barking. Phil walks away from Earl and answers the door. Frank
standing there. Phil looks a bit surprised and fumbles a moment...They stand in doorway
and speak very quietly;

PHIL
Hello. Frank. Frank TJ Mackey.

FRANK
...are you Phil...?

PHIL
Yeah. I was trying to get in touch with you. We got dissconnected.

FRANK
I got your message. That you were trying to get me -- right?

PHIL
Yes. I didn't know how to find you.
Earl asked me, so I looked through the adress books and there was no number, nothing
--

FRANK
Is Linda here?

PHIL
She's not here, she went out.
I'm sorry. This is all just so,
I don't know what, what to do -- your
Dad asked me to try and track you down.
To get you and I did, I called the number --
Do you wanna come in?

FRANK
Yeah let's...maybe just stand.

PHIL

These Dogs'll calm down -- you just have to come in --
He steps in the door and the dogs start to settle down a bit.

PHIL
He's in here.

FRANK
Let's just wait one minute and stay here, okay?

PHIL
Ok.
BEAT. They stand in the foyer and the dogs eventually calm down and go away. BEAT.

FRANK
How long have you taken care of him?

PHIL
For six months. I'm the day nurse...

FRANK
Uh-huh. What's going on?

PHIL
He's...I'm sorry...so sorry...I've seen this before, you know and you don't....
He's going very fast....Frank...um....

FRANK
Is he in pain?

PHIL
I just...he was...but I gave him,
I just had to give him a small dose of liquid morphine. He hasn't been able to swallow
the morphine pills so we now,
I just had to go to the liquid morphine...
For the pain, you understand?

FRANK
...uh-huh...
BEAT. Silence, then:

FRANK
How long...you think?

PHIL
Um...soon tonight...I think, yes?
Tommorrow...I mean...very soon...very...

FRANK
When did he go off chemo?

PHIL
About three weeks ago.

FRANK
.....have you ever seen this..I mean, never mind, you said --

PHIL
I work as a nurse, for a proffesion --

FRANK
Uh. huh.

PHIL
I'm really sorry.

FRANK
He's in here --?

PHIL
Yeah.
Phil starts to guide him, Frank holds him back.

FRANK
No, let's just wait one minute, let's just stand here one minute or so --
BEAT. They stand. HOLD.

PHIL
I've heard your tapes on the phone.

FRANK
Oh yeah.

PHIL
When they put me on hold, to talk to you...they play the tapes.
I mean: I'd seen the commercials and heard about you, but I'd never heard the tapes ....

FRANK
Uh. huh.

PHIL
It's interesting.

FRANK
Mmm.
Long pause. Then:

CUT TO:
INT. LAMPLIGHTER - THAT MOMENT
CAMERA with Stanley, sitting alone in a booth with a Coke and a cookie.
He's reading a book. BEAT, HOLD, THEN:
CAMERA pans/dollies away and booms up -- moving across the restaraunt -- across the way, sitting in a booth by the opposite window, out of view from Stanley;
Dixon, the little kid from earlier, sitting in a booth with a young black male, WORM (20s) This is clearly the back figure we've been seeing glimpses of --

ANGLE, AT THE BOOTH.
Dixon eats same pudding. Worm mumbles to him, various jabs.
"...sit up straight..." "...world is hard..." "..little brat..."
HOLD. Worm glances across the coffee shop -- he sees Stanley.
Worm HOLDS his look, thinks a moment. He looks up at the
WOMAN behind the counter...she's doing a crossword puzzle.
Worm looks back to Dixon, subtle mumbles and gestures and few moments later, Dixon stands from the booth and exits the coffee shop.
HOLD w/WORM. He sticks a finger down his throat, makes himself well with tears.
He stands up OUT OF FRAME.

ANGLE, COUNTER NEAR STANLEY.
Worm sits into FRAME, near to Stanley. Stanley glances up, they make a quick moment of eye contact, then look away. BEAT. HOLD.

CUT TO:
EXT. PARKING LOT/BEHIND LAMPLIGHTER - MOMENTS LATER
CAMERA follows Dixon as he walks towards an old beat up PARKED CAR.
He stops, hesitates, looks across the way --
LINDA'S MERCEDES is parked.
He hestitates a moment, looks left and right and all around and then he starts to walk over to the car...
AT LINDA'S CAR. Dixon sees that she's passed out, knocks on the window...

DIXON
Lady...hey Lady...Lady....you ok? you alive...huh...hey?
He looks around again, then gets in the passenger's side of the car, shakes her same more.

DIXON
Lady. Lady. Hey wake up. Lady?
Dixon reaches down and takes her PURSE, takes the MONEY out of the
WALLET and then reaches for her CEL PHONE and dials 911.

DIXON
Hello? Hello? I have an emergency situation -- this lady -- this lady seems like she's
dead -- hello?
She's in the parking lot -- (etc. gives information regarding location. etc.)
Then he gets out, walks back across parking lot...and into the concealed parked car he
came from --

CUT TO:
INT. JIMMY'S HOUSE - LIVING ROOM - THAT MOMENT
Jimmy and Rose. They're on the couch. Lights dim. Sitting, talking.
She hands him a pill from a bottle with a drink.

JIMMY
I don't think I want that.

ROSE
It'll take the pain away.

JIMMY
It's not really pain.
She sets it on the coffee table. Drinks a drink herself.

JIMMY
I gotta ask you for a cigarette, 'cause
I don't wanna spend six hours tryin' to get it to my mouth --
She lights a cigarette, puts it in his hand and he struggles a bit with his hand/eye
coordination....beat, then;

JIMMY
How do we do this, then?

ROSE
We just do it...we do it and we figure it out and we do as we do, I guess...

JIMMY
Do you love me, Rose?
She smiles and moves closer to him.

ROSE
You're my handsome man.

JIMMY
I'm a bad person.

ROSE

No. No.

JIMMY
No, I mean: I'm telling you this, now.
You see? You see I want to make everything clear and clean...and apologize for me....for all the stupid things I've done....that will eat me up....

ROSE
You feel like you want to be forgiven for your sins? Honey, you're not on your death bed, yet....this kinda talk's gonna get you in trouble --

JIMMY
--- don't. don't. Please. Just... listen to me...honey....
(beat)
...I've done...I've cheated on you.
Rose doesn't move much. Hold.

JIMMY
I've cheated on you and it kills me and the guilt of what I've done...I don't want you to think...maybe you knew,
I think that maybe you've known...
So I hope that I'm not saying this for me...for me to make myself feel better about what I've done...but for making you not feel like you're sitting there like a jerk...you've been the good one...
You understand...I'm so sorry for all I've done wrong...and this is pathetic...what?
"Dying man, confess the sins" something?
Is it selfish for me to say this? To say what I've done...I feel better already.
I do...do you hate me?
Rose takes a long moment, then:

ROSE
...No...I don't hate you.
(beat)
Do you want talk...do you really want to talk to me and say things and get things figured out, Jimmy?

JIMMY
Yeah.

ROSE
The question isn't wether or not you cheated on me, the question is how many times have you cheated on me?

JIMMY
Will that help?

ROSE
Yeah.

CUT TO:
INT. BILLINGSLEY'S - THAT MOMENT
In a secluded table in this dark steak place. Jim Kurring and
Claudia. CAMERA does a slow push in on a 2-shot.

CLAUDIA
Did you ever go out with someone and just....lie....question after question, maybe you're trying to make yourself look cool or better than you are or whatever, or smarter or cooler and you just -- not really lie, but maybe you just don't say everything --

JIM KURRING
Well, that's a natural thing, two people go out on a date, something. They want to impress people, the other person...or they're scared maybe what they say will make the other person not like them --

CLAUDIA
So you've done it --

JIM KURRING
Well I don't go out very much.

CLAUDIA
Why not?

JIM KURRING
I've never found someone really that
I think I would like to go out with.

CLAUDIA
And I bet you say that to all the girls --

JIM KURRING
No, no.

CLAUDIA
You wanna make a deal with me?

JIM KURRING ok.

CLAUDIA
What I just said...y'know, people afraid to say things....no guts to say the things that they...that are real or something...

JIM KURRING
...yeah...

CLAUDIA
To not do that. To not do that that we've maybe done -- before --

JIM KURRING
Let's make a deal.

CLAUDIA
Ok. I'll tell you everything and you tell me everything and maybe we can get through
all the piss and shit and lies that kill other people....
He laughs a bit uncomfortable...repeats her line;

JIM KURRING
Wow....huh..."...piss and shit..."

CLAUDIA
What?

JIM KURRING
You really use strong language.

CLAUDIA
I'm sorry --

JIM KURRING
-- no, no, it's fine. Fine.

CLAUDIA
I didn't mean...it's seems vulgar or something, I know --

JIM KURRING
It's fine.

CLAUDIA
I'm sorry.

JIM KURRING
...nothing. I'm sorry...

CLAUDIA
No, I'm sorry. I'm saying I'm sorry.
I talk like a jerk sometimes --

JIM KURRING

-- well I'm a real...y'know, straight when it comes to that...curse words
I just don't use much --

CLAUDIA
I'm sorry.

BEAT.
CLAUDIA
I'm gonna run to the bathroom for a minute...maybe just --

JIM KURRING ok.

CLAUDIA ok.
She goes. HOLD with him for a moment.

CUT TO:
EXT. SOLOMON and SOLOMON ELECTRONICS - THAT MOMENT
CAMERA is around back with Donnie in the Buick Regal.
He parks, gets out, looks around the empty place.
CAMERA tracks with him toWards a back loading dock area.
He puts a large HAT on his head, to cover his face.
He takes one of the KEYS from the key chain and uses it to get in a door in back. He
enters.

CUT TO:
INT. SOLOMON AND SOLOMON ELECTRONICS - THAT MOMENT
Donnie in a back corridor. He walks down through some BOXES and assorted
MERCHANDISE towards another door. He pulls his hat down some more, moves
swiftly.
He arrives at another door and does a KEY PAD CODE thing and also uses ANOTHER
KEY from the key chain.

ANOTHER BACK CORRIDOR
Donnie enters, walks towards Solomon's office and does another
Key Pad Code and Lock thing and enters --

SOLOMON'S OFFICE
Donnie enters, takes a quick beeline to behind the desk and under the floor, under a rug
he kneels down....

DONNIE'S POV he pulls the rug back and there's a SAFE. He does the combination
and opens it up.

IN THE SAFE.
There's five stacks of five thousand dollars for a total of
$25,000. In addition, some jewelry and some papers, etc.

CU - DONNIE he starts to take the money, putting into a plastic shopping bag.

CUT TO:
INT. EARL'S HOUSE - THAT MOMENT
Frank and Phil stand in the foyer. They're quiet a moment, then:

FRANK
So....Phil....um...I think I'm gonna step in and try and see him and say something if he can...talk...I mean:

PHIL
...ok...

FRANK
Can you stand...back...maybe, I mean... just a little bit...in the room is ok, but back from us a little...

PHIL yeah.
Frank walks slowly into the Living Room and over to Earl's bedside. He's holding back his tears. He sits. Earl is eyes closed, breathing a bit irregular....HOLD.

FRANK
...Dad...Dad...hey...Earl?
He tries to wake him a bit, but Earl is not moving.

FRANK
...hey...Dad...Dad can you wake up a minute Dad?
He turns to Phil, crying now, says:

FRANK
He's not waking up.

CUT TO:
INT. JIMMY'S HOUSE - THAT MOMENT
CAMERA holds CU on Jimmy.

ROSE
How many times....it's ok...just say...
Just say...

JIMMY
I don't even remember...many...twenty... maybe more...not much more...twenty times.

BEAT.
ROSE

I don't hate you, Jimmy. But I have a couple questions that I wanna ask....

JIMMY
I'll answer anything.

ROSE
Was there anyone that I know?

JIMMY
Yes.

ROSE
Who?

JIMMY
Rose, I don't --

ROSE hey.

JIMMY
Paula. Ellen.
She laughs a bit, rolls her eyes.

JIMMY
That's it.

ROSE
No one else that I know?

JIMMY
No.

ROSE
How long with Ellen?

JIMMY
Just once.

ROSE
How long with Paula?

JIMMY
Two years...three years...

ROSE
What about now?

JIMMY
It's over. I talked to her this morning.

ROSE
Is it over 'cause you're sick?

JIMMY
It's over becuase...for all the the right reasons I hope, what I said.

ROSE
Do you have any children with anyone?

JIMMY
What? No, Rose, jesus, no --

ROSE
Well maybe.

JIMMY
I don't.

ROSE
Do you feel better now that you've said this?

JIMMY
I don't know....

ROSE
I'm not mad. I am, but I'm not. Y'know?

JIMMY
I love you so much.

ROSE
I'm not through asking my questions.
Jimmy laughs a bit, smiles.

ROSE
Why doesn't Claudia talk to you, Jimmy?

JIMMY
Why, well I think we've, we both don't know...what do you mean?

ROSE
I think that you know.

JIMMY
Maybe...I don't...

BEAT. HOLD.
CUT TO:
EXT. VENTURA BLVD. - THAT MOMENT
CAMERA tracks with an AMBULANCE rushing down the street.

CUT TO:
INT. LAMPLIGHTER - THAT MOMENT
Through the window, the AMBULANCE passes in the b.g., heading nearby...and OC
we hear the siren throughout scene;
Stanley looks up at Worm, who's crying harder now, they make another moment of eye
contact. BEAT, THEN:

WORM
Hi.

STANLEY
Hi.

WORM
..sorry...

STANLEY
It's ok.

BEAT.
STANLEY
Are you alright?
Worm looks up.

CUT TO:
EXT. EMPTY PARKING LOT - THAT MOMENT
The AMBULANCE arrives at Linda's Mercedes and the PARAMEDICS hop out, open
the doors, call direction and try to speak with her and revive, etc. CAMERA is HAND
HELD and moving frantically with them;
PARAMEDICS (various)
Hello, hello, can you hear us, huh?
Stay with us, can you hear me...etc. etc.

ANGLE, ACROSS THE PARKING LOT.
Dixon is hiding way across the way in the shadowed, hidden parked car, watching the
paramedics. All the while he counts the money from Linda's wallet.

CUT TO:
INT. BILLINGSLEY'S BATHROOM - THAT MOMENT.
CAMERA with Claudia, she snorts some coke off her hand in the stall.
She takes a quick look in the mirror, walks out --

CUT TO:
INT. BILLINGSLEY'S - THAT MOMENT
CAMERA tracks with Claudia as she walks back to the table...she comes up from behind Jim Kurring and leans in quick...KISSES
HIM ON THE CHEEK and then quickly sits down across from him;

CLAUDIA
I wanted to do that.
Jim Kurring smiles, shaken a bit.

JIM KURRING
Well.

CLAUDIA
That felt good to do...to do what
I wanted to do.

JIM KURRING
Yeah.

CLAUDIA
Can I tell you something?

JIM KURRING
Yeah, of course.

CLAUDIA
I'm really nervous that you're gonna hate me soon. That you're gonna find stuff out about me and you're gonna hate me --

JIM KURRING
-- no, like what, what do you mean?

CLAUDIA
You're a police officer. You have so much, so many good things and you seem so together...so all straight and put together without problems.

JIM KURRING
I lost my gun.

CLAUDIA

What?

JIM KURRING
I lost my gun after I left you today and I'm the laughing stock of a lot of people. I wanted to tell you that.
I wanted you to know...and it's on my mind and it makes me look like a fool and
I feel like a fool and you asked that we should say things, that we should say what we're thinknig and not lie about things and I'll tell you that, this: that I lost my gun and I'm not a good cop...and I'm looked down at...and I know that....and I'm scared that once you find that out you might not like me.

CLAUDIA
Oh my god, Jim. Jim, that was so --

JIM KURRING
I'm sorry --

CLAUDIA
That was so great what you just said.

JIM KURRING
I haven't been on a date since I was married and that was three years ago....and Claudia...whatever you wanna tell me, whatever you think might scare me, won't...and I will listen...I will be a good listener to you if that's what you want...and you know, you know...I won't judge you....
I can do that sometimes, I know, but
I won't...I can...listen to you and you shouldn't be scared of scaring me off or anything that you might think I'll think or on and on and just say it and
I'll listen to you....

CLAUDIA
You don't how fuckin' stupid I am.

JIM KURRING
It's ok.

CLAUDIA
You don't know how crazy I am.

JIM KURRING
It's ok.

CLAUDIA
I've got troubles.

JIM KURRING

I'll take everything at face value.
I'll be a good listener to you.

CLAUDIA
Ohhhh I started this, didn't I, didn't I, didn't I, fuck.

JIM KURRING
Say what you want and you'll see --

CLAUDIA
Wanna kiss me, Jim?

JIM KURRING
Yes I do.
They lean across the table and kiss each other. CAMERA DOLLIES
IN SUPER QUICK as their lips touch.

CUT TO:
INT. SOLOMON AND SOLOMON ELCTRONICS - THAT MOMENT
Donnie finishes taking the money from the safe....
...Donnie walks back one of the corridors and heads through a door...(again using the key and code)....
...Donnie enters into the warehouse area and heads for the door to outside....
...He puts the key into the lock and opens the door....but he takes a small stumble back and the key chain that's attached to his belt gets stuck, causing him to fall back, down and to the ground...with the KEY SNAPPING OFF IN THE LOCK....
..the door is about to shut on him but he stops it with his foot....he gets up, grabs the money...leaves with the broken key still left in the lock...

CUT TO:
EXT. SOLOMON AND SOLOMON PARKING LOT - THAT MOMENT
Donnie gets in the Buick Regal and drives away.

CUT TO:
EXT. EMPTY PARKING LOT/LINDA'S MERCEDES - THAT MOMENT
CAMERA (HAND HELD) is in the middle of the PARAMEDICS dealing with Linda....they find the pill bottle...they put her on a gurney...they search for ID, come up only with the registration for the car and some papers in the glove box....they get her into the ambulance....

CUT TO:
INT. LAMPLIGHTER - THAT MOMENT
Stanley finishes his cookie. Worm, sitting across from him starts to cry a little, very quietly. He hides it best he can.
Stanley looks up here and there from his books. They make another moment of eye contact then:

WORM
Hi.

STANLEY
Hi.

WORM
..sorry...

STANLEY
It's ok.

BEAT.
STANLEY
Are you alright?
Worm looks up.

CUT TO:
INT. JIMMY'S HOUSE - THAT MOMENT
Jimmy and Rose. HOLD. THEN:

ROSE
...say it, Jimmy...

JIMMY
Do you know the answer to this?

ROSE
I'm asking you. I'm asking you if you know why Clauida will not speak to you....please,
Jimmy....tell me.

JIMMY
I think that she thinks I may have molested her.
Rose doesn't flinch.

JIMMY
She thinks terrible things that somehow got in her head...that I might have done
something. She said that to me last time...when it was...ten years ago she walked out the
door,
"You touched me wrong..." "I know that."
Some crazy thought in her, in her head...

ROSE
Did you ever touch her?

JIMMY
...No....
HOLD. BEAT. Rose asks again;

ROSE
Jimmy, did you touch her?

JIMMY
I don't know.
Rose starts to cry a bit. So does Jimmy.

ROSE
...Jimmy...

JIMMY
I really don't know.

ROSE
But you can't say....

JIMMY
I don't know what I've done.

ROSE
Yes you do....you do and you won't say.

JIMMY
...I don't know...
She stands up and walks to a small table and gets her car keys and her jacket....

JIMMY
What...? ...no...no, please...
She stands above him.

ROSE
You deserve to die alone for what you've done.

JIMMY
I don't know what I've done.

ROSE
Yes you do.

JIMMY
Stay here, please don't leave me, please, please, if I said I knew would you stay?

ROSE
No.

JIMMY
I don't know what I've done.

ROSE
You should know better.
She leaves.

CUT TO:
INT. BILLINGSLEY'S - THAT MOMENT
CAMERA CU on Claudia as she pulls back from the kiss. HOLD.
She starts to cry....through her tears, then:

CLAUDIA
....now that I've met you....
Would you object to never seeing me again?

CU. JIM
JIM KURRING
What?

CLAUDIA
Just say no.

JIM KURRING
I won't say, no, wait, Claudia --
ECU - The two of them. Tight, tight 2-shot. She gets up and walks out, he follows --
grabs her arm and she whispers, forcefully:

CLAUDIA
Let me go, leave me, let me go, it's ok, please.

JIM KURRING please, what is it, please --

CLAUDIA just let me walk out, ok?
She leaves in tears. He watches her walk.

CUT TO:
EXT. VENTURA BLVD. - THAT MOMENT
CAMERA is travelling with the PARAMEDICS who are driving real fast.
They approach a RED LIGHT at an intersection....
....they breeze through it, but the CAMERA PANS and moves over to
Donnie's BUICK REGAL that's stopped at the intersection....
CAMERA moves into a CU of him behind the wheel. He's paniced. HOLD.

DONNIE

What am I doing? What am I doing?

What the fuck am I doing?

Donnie looks at the large bag of money in the passenger's seat next to him...he panics same more...

DONNIE

WHAT THE FUCK AM I DOING?

WIDE ANGLE, THAT MOMENT

Donnie's Buick Regal makes a u-turn and heads back the direction it came ---

CUT TO:

INT. EARL'S HOUSE - THAT MOMENT

Frank and Earl. Earl opens his eyes a bit.

FRANK

Dad...dad it's me...it's Frank...

It's Jack....It's Jack....Dad....

Earl can barely make it but he touches Frank....Frank holds his Dad's hand....Phil steps up closer....

FRANK

I'm here. I'm here now. What do you want?

Do you want anything?

PHIL

I don't think, he can't...

FRANK

...just wait...Dad...you want something...can you say...

EARL

.....fuck...fuck...fuck...

Earl is in PAIN and his hallucination make him a bit angry.

EARL

...thismssm....

FRANK

Oh, Dad. It's ok. jesus. ok. it's ok...I'm here with you now, please. i'm sorry...it's ok. alright..ok.

CUT TO:

EXT. VENTURA BLVD - THAT MOMENT

CAMERA with the Buick Regal. It moves past CAMERA, which PANS and DOLLIES over to --

THE LAMPLIGHTER COFFEE SHOP. Looking inside, through the window to see Stanley and Worm, sitting talking...

CAMERA GOES INSIDE THE LAMPLIGHTER COFFEE SHOP.
QUICK DISSOLVE TO:

INT. LAMPLIGHTER - THAT MOMENT
Worm is in tears, talking to Stanley. SLOW ZOOM IN.

WORM
....you have it...easy....you know?
You have a father who loves you, huh?

STANLEY
Yes.

WORM
You know what it's like to come home scared, scared that maybe if you don't have the money you're supposed to go out each day and get that you're gonna get beaten....by a belt...he hits me with a belt, Stanley....
(beat)
I'm supposed to sell those candy bars, and if I don't, I come home without the money....

STANLEY
....Why does he do it...?

WORM
Cause he hates me....he hates me so much.

STANLEY
It's not right.

WORM
I hate it.
CU - Worm. He hesitates...looks at Stanley and says:

WORM
I'm sorry to put all this on you, Stanley --

STANLEY
I have money.

WORM
...what...?

STANLEY
I have money to give you.

WORM
No. No. I have to do this on my own.

STANLEY
I can take you to get money. I don't need it...I don't need it -- listen to me:
I can let you have money so your father won't hit you ever again -- you'll have the money
because I don't need it.
CAMERA pushes in a little on Worm, he looks up. 30fps.

WORM
Where do you have it?
CAMERA holds 2-shot, looking out the window onto the street.
We PUSH PAST THEM AND THROUGH THE WINDOW, picking up with a
YELLOW CAB as it drives by, PAN with it....

QUICK DISSOLVE TO:
EXT. VENTURA BLVD. - THAT MOMENT
CAMERA travels with the CAB for a moment or two...CAMERA goes inside the
CAB....

QUICK DISSOLVE TO:
INT. CAB - MOVING - THAT MOMENT
CAMERA is in the back with CLAUDIA. She slouches down. She's still crying...she
snorts some coke off her hand....

CUT TO:
EXT. VENTURA BLVD. - THAT MOMENT
CAMERA moves with the CAB a bit....it makes a right hand turn and the CAMERA
PANS and DOLLIES away, over towards a JAGUAR stopped at the intersection....it's
making a left turn at the intersection, going the same way as the CAB did....we push in
close and land to see ROSE behind the wheel....She's in tears....
Light turns from RED to GREEN.

CUT TO:
INT. JIMMY'S HOUSE - THAT MOMENT
Jimmy, without a real trace of coordination walks from the living room and into

THE KITCHEN
He moves to a drawer and removes a REVOLVER. His hand is shaking and his
hand/eye coordination makes it very hard to grasp hold, but he finally does....he's
shaking and tearing....

CUT TO:

EXT. BILLINGSLEY'S PARKING LOT - THAT MOMENT
CAMERA tracks with Jim Kurring to his car. He gets behind the wheel.

CUT TO:
EXT. INTERSECTION - MOMENTS LATER
CAMERA overhead as Jim Kurring's car drives past the Magnolia/Tujunga intersection....

CUT TO:
INT. JIM KURRING'S CAR - MOVING - THAT MOMENT
CU - Jim Kurring driving. HOLD. He drives past Solomon and
Solomon Electronics.....

JIM'S POV - THAT MOMENT - MOVING he sees the parked Buick Regal and
Donnie (in shadow) get out and head for the back door....
CU - Kurring. He registers what he saw.

CUT TO:
EXT. SOLOMON AND SOLOMON/LOADING DOCK AREA - THAT MOMENT
CAMERA moves with Donnie over to the back door...he reaches down to his KEY
CHAIN and sees:
The BROKEN KEY....it's snapped off the key chain....one half remains....the other half
is on the other side of the door in the lock....

DONNIE
Fuck.

CUT TO:
INT. JIM KURRING'S CAR - THAT MOMENT Sequence J
Jim Kurring drives a few more feet....slows down...then starts to make a u-turn to go
back to the store....

JIM'S POV - MOVING - THROUGH THE WINDHSIELD.
The car starts to turn 180 degrees......as soon as it is headed going back the opposite
direction....

........CRACK........
From the sky, out of the blue, a large GREEN FROG lands on Jim Kurring's windhsield.
CU - Jim Kurring. Scared shitless.
POV - Another GREEN FROG slams on the HOOD OF THE CAR.
CU - Brake. Jim's foot SLAMS ON THE BRAKE.

CUT TO:
EXT. MAGNOLIA BLVD. - THAT MOMENT
CAMERA holds a wide angle as Jim Kurring's CAR SLAMS AND SKIDS TO

A STOP IN THE MIDDLE OF THE EMPTY STREET.
CLOSER ANGLE, PUSH IN ON THE DRIVER'S SIDE WINDOW.
Jim is scared and sweating.....he looks up, out the driver's side window....

JIM'S POV - LOOKING STRAIGHT UP.
It's dark and empty sky.....
....hold on him....he looks at the Frog that has landed on the windshield....it's dead and splattered.....

SUDDENLY:
The SOUND of ANOTHER FROG FALLING FROM THE SKY AND SLAMMING

ON THE ROOF OF THE CAR.
Jim jumps.....looks up again....
....from straight out of the sky comes ANOTHER FROG falling
DIRECTLY INTO THE CAMERA....it SPLATS....
...then another and another and another.....

WIDE ANGLE. THE STREET.
It starts to RAIN FROGS in the middle of Magnolia Blvd.

CUT TO:
INT. CLAUDIA'S APARTMENT
CU - Claudia snorts a line of coke off her coffee table.
She comes up and INTO FRAME. Outside the window, behind her....
...a FROG FALLS straight past.....
She hears the sound and turns around....sees nothing...
CU - Profile on Clauida....through the other window...another
FROG falls past, through the tree outside on it's way down.....
She turns her head again sees nothing....

BEAT.
Another FROG FALLS...she looks...she walks to the window....
.....A dozen FROGS FALL IN VERY QUICK SUCCESION.....
She jumps back from the window...stumbles a bit...knocks over a lamp, which
SMASHES to the floor.....her apartment goes DARK....except for street light...more
FROGS FALL and we hear the sound and see them through the window in glimpses.....

CUT TO:
EXT. CLAUDIA'S APARTMENT/STREET - THAT MOMENT
The FROGS are falling sort of heavy now....Rose's JAGUAR comes through it....skids
and SMASHES into a PARKED CAR....
CAMERA DOLLIES over to her....she looks up at them....they FALL

**STRAIGHT INTO CAMERA AND ONTO THE HOOD, WINDSHIELD AND
ROOF....**

..Rose puts the Jaguar in reverse and tries to back away from the smashed parked car.....the bumper's are stuck....

CUT TO:
INT. EARL'S HOUSE - THAT MOMENT
The CAMERA holds on Earl and Frank. Frank has his head buried in Earl's bed holding his hand, crying....it's very quiet....
CU - Phil. He's crying a bit standing off to the side.
He looks out the window's and the glass doors and sees the FROGS come raining down. His mouth drops and he can't speak.
Frank doesn't notice. The FROGS fall in the backyard and into THE POOL.

PHIL
There are frogs falling from the sky.

CUT TO:
EXT. WHITSETT/NORTH HOLLYWOOD MED. CENTER - THAT MOMENT
The PARAMEDICS are driving real fast down the street.....

CUT TO:
INT. AMBULANCE - MOVING - THAT MOMENT
Linda is on life support stuff in the ambulance. Looking past her, we see the view of the road through the windshield -- the amubulance driver going real fast and just about to pull into the hospital emergency entrance....

FROGS START PELTING THE WINDSHIELD.....THE DRIVER SWERVES...
CUT TO:
EXT. STREET/AMBULANCE - THAT MOMENT
A WIDE ANGLE where we see the FROGS falling onto the moving, swerving Ambulance....one FROG lands so hard on top of the red lights on the ambulance that it CRACKS....
...the FROGS in the middle of the road start to act as a lubricant on the already wet/damp street and the Ambulance starts to SKID SIDEWAYS....
...it FALLS ON IT'S SIDE.

CUT TO:
INT. AMBULANCE - POV
As it falls on it's side and skids a bit....over the Frogs...

CUT TO:
EXT. EMERGENCY ROOM ENTRANCE - THAT MOMENT
Ambulance skids right up to the emergency room entrance.

CUT TO:
INT. JIMMY'S HOUSE - KITCHEN - THAT MOMENT
Jimmy with the Revolver to his head...he cocks it back...

INTERCUT:
EXT. SKY/INT. HOUSE - THAT MOMENT
CAMERA above Jimmy's house, looking straight down and MOVING towards a SKYLIGHT above the kitchen...a FROG enters FRAME, falling straight towards this skylight --
Inside the house,
Jimmy about to pull the trigger...SOUND DROPS OUT.
The falling FROG comes STRAIGHT THROUGH THE SKYLIGHT, SMASHING

THROUGH....
...falls straight down onto Jimmy's head....the GUN GOES OFF
WILDLY.....SMASHES the TELEVISION.......
Jimmy falls to the ground....GLASS FALLS from the broken skylight....
...more FROGS continue to fall through it and into the kitchen and around Jimmy.....
...the BULLET into TELEVISION has sparked something and the SOCKET it's plugged into CATCHES FIRE.....

CU - INSIDE THE WALL, NEAR THE SOCKET.
Camera moves in and sees some SPARK and FLASH and FIRE started....

CUT TO:
EXT. SOLOMON AND SOLOMON ELECTRONICS - THAT MOMENT
Donnie starts to climb up a ladder attached to the side of the building....near the loading dock area....

CUT TO:
EXT. STREET NEARBY - THAT MOMENT
Jim Kurring is in the middle of the Frog Rain...he puts his car into gear and drives down the street....
....about twenty yards later and he's out of it....
...he pulls into the parking lot behind Solomon and
Solomon.....it's not raining frogs here.....
Kurring's HEADLIGHTS catch a glimpse of Donnie starting to climb...
...Donnie gets scared and FREEZES....
...Kurring is oblivious to Donnie for the moment. He looks in his REARVIEW MIRROR and sees the FROGS FALLING....
...Donnie looks past Kurring and now sees the FROGS FALLING in a 50 x 50 area in the street....
...Donnie looks up...

....FROGS ARE FALLING STAIGHT AT HIM/CAMERA AND THEY KNOCK HIM DOWN
AND TO THE CEMENT.....he falls flat on his FACE...
...Jim Kurring turns his head and sees Donnie, fallen flat face and bloody on the pavement....he gets out of his car and runs over to Donnie, through the Frogs that rain

down, and picks him/drags him out of harm and under shelter in the LOADING DOCK AREA.

CUT TO:
INT. CLAUDIA'S APARTMENT - THAT MOMENT
CAMERA (STEADICAM) follows ROSE as she runs up the stairs to Claudia's place and frantically BANGS ON THE DOOR...
Inside the apartment, Claudia JUMPS and SCREAMS at the sound....

ROSE
HONEY, HONEY, CLAUDIA. IT'S ME.
IT'S MOM. MOM. OPEN THE DOOR.
OPEN YOUR DOOR HONEY.
Claudia jumps up and goes to her door in the darkness and opens it up -- Rose comes in quick, scared shitless...they fall down and hold onto each other, sweatin/crying/shaking....

CUT TO:
INT. EARL'S HOUSE - THAT MOMENT
Frank lifts his head and watches the FROGS FALL outside the house.
Earl looks to Frank....he musters something...Frank notices....
All SOUND DROPS OUT except for the breathing of Frank and Earl.

EARL
You are not what you think you are.
Frank breaks down.

CUT TO:
INT. LAMPLIGHTER - THAT MOMENT
Stanley and Worm. CAMERA holds as all around...through the glass windows...it RAINS FROGS....smashing to the ground.....hitting a couple odd parked cars...they sit, watching, stunned...in a sort of daze.
Stanley seems almost happy. Worm shocked, scarred;

WORM
What is that?

STANLEY
It's frogs. It's raining frogs.

WORM
...fuck you mean, it's raining frogs?

STANLEY
It's raining frogs from the sky.

WORM
....what the fuck, what the fuck....

STANLEY
This happens....this is something that happens.

WORM
What the fuck is goin' on, WHAT THE

FUCK IS GOING ON?
CU - STANLEY. HOLD ON HIS FACE extremely tight.
In the reflection of his eye, we see the Frogs falling.... past the neon sign that reads
"Fresh Coffee."
ANGLE, DIXON. He comes running into the Lamplighter and over to Worm and
Stanley....he's scarred shitless and frantic --

DIXON
DADDY! DAD! DAD WHAT THE HELL IS GOIN' ON?
WORM
Stay quiet...stay quiet, son --

DIXON
LET'S GO, LET'S GO, LET'S GET HIS MONEY
AND GO -- DID YOU GET HIS MONEY? DID
YOU GET IT? DID YOU GET HIS MONEY, DAD?
WORM
No, Son...be quiet...be quiet now...

DIXON
C'mon, Dad. We gotta just GET HIS
MONEY AND GO, LET'S GO. Let's get the money --

WORM
We're not gonna do that now. We're not gonna do that now and that's over.

DIXON
BULLSHIT. BULLSHIT, DAD WE NEED
TO GET HIS MONEY AND GO.
Dixon takes out a large POLICE ISSUED REVOLVER, AIMS at STANLEY'S FACE.

DIXON
GIVE US YOUR MONEY MAN.
WORM
Son, don't --

DIXON

**BULLSHIT, BULLSHIT DAD WE GOTTA GET
HIS MONEY --**
WORM
-- no.

DIXON
(to Stanley)

GIVE US YOUR MONEY.
WORM
Put the gun down, please, boy.

DIXON
GIVE US YOUR MONEY, KID.
WORM
Son, please, now....

DIXON
DAD --
WORM
Please, boy, put it down and it's ok.
Dixon starts to get nervous and well with tears...he shakes a little....

WORM
It's ok --

DIXON
We gotta get his money so we can get outta here -- we gotta --

WORM
That idea is over now.
We're not gonna do that now.
Dixon starts crying and shaking and backing away --

DIXON
DADDY, FUCK, DADDY, DON'T GET MAD AT ME.
DON'T GET MAD AT ME --
(to Stanley)

JUST GIMME YOUR MONEY.
WORM
I'm not mad, son, I will not be mad at you and it's ok and please put it down and I won't
be mad and I won't --

DIXON
DAD.

Dixon starts to lower the gun a bit, crying and shaking....He lowers the gun and hands it over to his Father....Dixon is sort of flinching....the possibility that his Father may strike him...
...Stanley is frozen...Dixon is hyperventilating....

DIXON
I - just - thought - that - I - didn't want - I - didn't - I - didn't -

WORM
It's ok, boy.
HOLD. Que. "Bein Green," by Kermit the Frog/Aimee

CUT TO:
EXT. LAMPLIGHTER/VENTURA BLVD. - THAT MOMENT Sequence K
CAMERA holds a wide angle on the Lamplighter Coffee Shop.
Frogs falling from sky onto and around the streets....

CUT TO:
EXT. THE SKY - THAT MOMENT
CAMERA up with the Falling Frogs....CAMERA is moving down with them... it becomes almost musical....like Busby-Berkely-style coreography of
Frogs That Fall In The Sky...

MUSIC/KERMIT THE FROG
"It's not that easy bein' green...
Having to spend each day the color of the leaves..."

CARRIES OVER CUT TO:
INT. JIMMY'S HOUSE - THAT MOMENT
It is on FIRE now....CU image of Jimmy on the floor of the kitchen with shards of glass around him...and FROGS...a few of them still alive and jumping around...the FIRE moving closer and closer...

CUT TO:
EXT. SOLOMON AND SOLOMON/LOADING DOCK AREA - THAT MOMENT
Jim Kurring and Donnie underneath the shelter area. Donnie's
MOUTH IS FULL OF BLOOD and his TEETH ARE BROKEN...

DONNIE
My teeff...my teeef....

JIM KURRING
YOU'RE OK...you're gonna be ok....

CUT TO:
INT. CLAUDIA'S APARTMENT - THAT MOMENT

Claudia cries to her Mom. Rose holds her and they rock back and forth.... Claudia cries loud and over and over --
"Mommy...mommy...mom."
Rose calming her and petting her head, "It's ok."

CUT TO:
INT. EMERGENCY ROOM - THAT MOMENT
CAMERA is with Linda and DOCTORS as they PUMP HER STOMACH.
Follow the process and get to point where it's clear that she is going to make it, she will not die.

CUT TO:
INT. EARL'S HOUSE - THAT MOMENT
CAMERA w/Frank and Earl and Phil. Earl's last couple of breaths are short and quick...short and quick...short and quick...and then he dies.....his eyes are open.....

CUT TO:
EXT. SKY - THAT MOMENT
CAMERA moves down straight towards the ground...towards the Magnolia intersection with a LARGE FROG....right before it hits the pavement --

CUT TO BLACK.
Title Card Reads: So Now Then
- Replay Lumiere Footage from the opening of "Three Men Hung"
Green, Berry and Hill.
- Replay Delmer Darion in the tree and getting lifted out of the water.
- Replay Sydney Barringer jumping from building

NARRATOR
And there is the account of the hanging of three men....and a scuba diver and a suicide.....

CUT TO:
INT. EARL'S HOUSE - DAWN
The door is opened by Phil and two MORTUARY MEN in suits nod their heads. Phil lets them in.

NARRATOR
There are stories of coincidence and chance and intersections and strange things told and which is which and who only knows...

CUT TO:
INT. EARL'S HOUSE - LIVING ROOM - THAT MOMENT
Frank and Phil watch Earl get covered in a sheet and put on a stretcher. CAMERA moves around and finds the MORPHINE DOG placed on a stretcher, covered in a sheet. HOLD CU on PHIL and then Frank.

NARRATOR
...and we generally say, "Well if that was in movie I wouldn't believe it."

ANGLE, IN THE KITCHEN, MOMENTS LATER
Phil enters and answers the phone, "...hello...oh no...yes, yes..."
Phil looks to Frank --

CUT TO:
INT. HOSPITAL - DAWN
CAMERA looking down the long emergency room corridor as the doors open and Frank
enters and moves to the reception desk, asks some information --
CAMERA pans off him, and over to a room, looking through the door jam onto Linda
in bed. Her eyes a bit open, respiratory equipment attached to her. A DOCTOR standing
over her, calmly asking questions;

DOCTOR
Are you with us? Linda? Is it Linda?
She nods her head. Doctor continues talk, etc. Frank, from behind enters FRAME and
stands off nearby. MATCH TO DIXON'S FACE

OVER CUT TO:
NARRATOR
Someone's so and so meet someone else's so and so and so on --
EXT. EMPTY PARKING LOT AREA - DAWN
CU - Dixon as he gets into the old beat up car with Worm.
Their call pulls away and drives off. Dixon looks at Linda's Mercedes which is still
parked way across the lot -- they exit FRAME.

CUT TO:
EXT. MAGNOLIA - DAWN
Worm's car drives down the street. LONG LENS. ANGLE, at the car,
Dixon leans up and out the window a bit....he's got the gun wrapped in newspaper,
taking the fingerprints from the gun....he throws the POLICE ISSUED WEAPON from
the speeding car...

CUT TO:
INT. LAMPLIGHTER - DAWN
Stanley sits in the back of a squad car....an OFFICER watching him...probably supposed
to be comforting him, but instead drinking coffee, chating with other OFFICERS
questioning the coffee shop employees --

NARRATOR
And it is in the humble opinion of this narrator that these strange things happen all the
time....

Stanley gets out of the car and walks away, out of sight of all the officer's and people around...he just walks down the street....

CUT TO:
INT. SPECTOR HOUSE - RICK'S BEDROOM - DAWN
Stanley enters Rick's bedroom. Rick is asleep.

STANLEY
Dad...Dad.
Rick opens his eyes, but doesn't move.

STANLEY
You have to be nicer to me, Dad.

RICK
Go to bed.

STANLEY
I think that you have to be nicer to me.

RICK
Go to bed.
Stanley exits.

CUT TO:
EXT. JIMMY'S HOUSE - DAWN
CAMERA with Fire Trucks and County Coroner people. A body bag and a stretcher carrying JIMMY'S BODY come out of the house.

NARRATOR
...and so it goes and so it goes and the book says, "We may be through with the past, but the past is not through with us."

CUT TO:
INT. POLICE STATION - MARCIE
Marcie looking down at the table in front of her, tape recorder and microphone in front of her, (and all that goes along w/full confession/etc.)

MARCIE
I killed him. I killed my husband.
He hit my son and he hit my grandson and I hit him. I hit him with the ashtray and he was knocked out and I killed him,
I strangled him. I strangled my husband to protect my boys. I protected my boys.

CUT TO:
EXT. SOLOMON AND SOLOMON - DAWN

Jim Kurring and Donnie sitting together at the loading dock.
Donnie, mouth full of blood, holding a kleenex to it, crying a bit.
Kurring listens. HOLD.

DONNIE
I know that I did a thtupid thing.
Tho-thtupid...getting brathes...I thought...
I thought that he would love me.
...getting brathes, for what... for thumthing I didn't even...i don't know where to put
things, y'know?
Kurring holds his look, nods. Donnie really breaks tears, looks up;

DONNIE
I really do hath love to give, I juth don't know where to put it --
CAMERA holds the 2-shot on them, BEAT, THEN: The Police Issued
Revolver FALLS FROM THE SKY AND LANDS ABOUT fifteen feet in front of
them. Jim Kurring and Donnie look. HOLD. CU - Jim Kurring.

CUT TO:
INT. SOLOMON AND SOLOMON ELECTRONICS - THAT MOMENT
Donnie and Jim Kurring walking inside the store, towards the office --

JIM KURRING
...these security systems can be a real joke.
I mean, a frog falls from the sky and lands on the x-4 box 'round back and opens all the
doors?
Triggers a siutation? You don't know who could be driving by at any moment, walk in
and rob the place -- I was you I'd talk to your boss about a new security system --

DONNIE
....ohh-thur-I-thur-thill....

JIM KURRING
You guys make alotta money, huh?

CUT TO:
INT. SOLOMON AND SOLOMON - OFFICE - MOMENT LATER
Donnie puts the money back in the floor safe. CU. DONNIE.

JIM KURRING (OC)
I got a buddy a mine down at the med. center, he'd probably do quite a deal on a set of
dentures, you're interested in that. He's in training, you know he's not a dentist yet, but
he's real good at corrective oral surgery from what I understand...
LAND ECU. DONNIE. He smiles a little bit.

CUT TO:

EXT. SOLOMON AND SOLOMON - THAT MOMENT
Wide Angle, Donnie and Jim Kurring shake hands and part ways, getting into their cars.
A few words more about, "Call me up for that guys number and he'll help you out with
the teeth."
Donnie gets in his car. CAMERA stays with Jim Kurring who walks over to his car and
gets behind the wheel.
CAMERA HOLDS ON HIM. He does a little "Cops" talking to himself.

JIM KURRING
...alot of people think this is just a job that you go to.....take a lunch hour, the jobs over,
something like that.
But...it's a 24 hour deal...no two ways about it....and what most people don't see: Just
How Hard It Is To Do The Right Thing.
(beat)
People think if I make a judgment call that it's a judgment on them...but that's not what
I do and that's not what should be done...I have to take everything and play it as it lays.
Sometimes people need a little help.
Sometimes people need to be forgiven and sometimes they need to go to jail.
And that's a very tricky thing on my part...making that call...the law is the law and heck
if I'm gonna break it...but you can forgive someone....? Well, that's the tough
part....What Do We Forgive?
Tough part of the job.....tough part of walking down the street...
CAMERA stays with him and HOLDS as he puts the car into gear and drives
away....HOLD with him as he drives...he starts to cry a little bit to himself.

CUT TO:
INT. CLAUDIA'S APARTMENT - THAT MOMENT
CAMERA holds on Claudia. She's sitting up in bed, covers around her, staring into
space....a SONG plays....for a very, very long time she doesn't move until she looks up
and sees someone enter her bedroom....a FIGURE from the back enters FRAME and
walks in and sits on the edge of the bed....from the back it is clear that it's Jim Kurring.
She tears a bit and looks at him...HOLD....
She turns her eyes from him and looks INTO THE CAMERA and smiles.

CUT TO BLACK.

END.